Our tow
DOVER
1945-2000

by

Derek Leach OBE and Terry Sutton MBE

Riverdale Publications, 24 Riverdale, River, Dover CT17 0QX

Dedicated to Trish Godfrey, Dover Public Library
Always so helpful

Published in 2003 by Riverdale Publications
24 Riverdale, River, Dover CT17 0QX

ISBN 0 9536166 4 9

Printed in England by A. R. Adams & Sons (Printers) Ltd.,
Dour Street, Dover, Kent CT16 1EW

CONTENTS

1940
PLAN
OF
DOVER
(PIKE'S BLUE BOOK SERIES)

INTRODUCTION

This book has its origins from a chance remark made by Trish Godfrey who manages the Local Studies Section of Dover Library. The Library receives many requests for information about Dover since 1945 and there are 'bits and pieces' in various books and files, but there is not one single book where the story of Dover since 1945 is dealt with comprehensively. This book aims to fill the gap not only for the benefit of pupils with local projects to complete and researchers present and future, but also for the entertainment and enjoyment of Dovorians who have lived through this period.

As well as covering all the important events and developments of these years the book encapsulates almost every aspect of life in the town including work, shopping and use of leisure in its many forms. An advantage in researching material has been that we have been able to contact people still living and we are very grateful to them for first-hand information. Many noteworthy characters span this period and a few have been highlighted.

Nobody can pretend that 1945 to 2000 was the greatest period in Dover's history and in many ways it was a disappointing and depressing time, but there were some dramatic developments such as the expansion of the port, the building and impact of the Channel Tunnel, the discovery of the Bronze Age Boat as well as the traumatic closure of the Kent Coalfield and the tragedies, particularly the loss of the *Herald of Free Enterprise*, the decline of our shopping centre and the failure 50 years after the Second World War to redevelop the bomb-damaged area of St James'.

At the end of the 20th century what was the state of Dover? In 1999 Dover District Council published economic and social information based on 1997 data for the whole District. In that year there were about 60,000 residents of working age in the District plus 25,000 children up to 17 years old and 23,000 over retirement age. Unemployment at 5.2% was double that of the South East region with 50% having only unskilled or no experience to offer. Wages were lower on average than in the South East generally and Dover had fewer highly skilled and more low skilled jobs compared with the rest of the UK. Parts of Dover were among the worst educationally in the South East. GCSE performance was in line with the national average but GCE A Level was below the Kent and England average. 80% of 16 year old pupils stayed on in full-time education. The deprivation ranking of Dover District worsened between 1994 and 1997 with parts of Dover categorised as very deprived. When the percentage of free school meals was taken as an indicator – 50% of children at some Dover schools were eligible compared with the Kent average of 16%. Almost 33% of Dover urban households claimed housing/council tax benefit. Recorded crime fell by almost 5% in 1998 with vehicle crime decreasing most and drug trafficking increasing. Dover town centre was the crime black spot followed by the port areas, Aycliffe, St Radigunds and Buckland.

There was also increasing public concern about antisocial behaviour, vandalism, litter and the depressing state of the town centre.

Dover has much to boast about, but we enter the 21st century facing a big challenge. There are now encouraging signs that the people of Dover are prepared to make the effort. Initiatives by The Dover Society and Town Centre Management, such as the Shop Watch, River Watch and Just Bin It campaigns, are catching the public's imagination. Whilst quite rightly taking great pride in our past, let us hope that we may soon be able to celebrate the Dover of today.

Derek Leach and Terry Sutton, 2003

Chapter 1

DOVER IN 1945

Dover emerged from the Second World War with pride, severely damaged by bombs and shells but winning the respect of the free world as Britain's front line town. The song *Bluebirds over the White Cliffs of Dover* made its name known worldwide. Large swathes were derelict, save for the remnants of war-wrecked homes and other property in much of the town centre. It felt eerie walking through once-densely populated parts, which now offered only the results of constant bombardment. Wallpaper peeled from interior walls while tar-covered fabric flapped in windows that no longer displayed glass. Butterflies fluttered around the buddleia that grew in profusion on bombsites and there was the unforgettable smell of abandoned homes and shops.

The Esplanade Hotel on the sea front – another war casualty

Throughout 1945 the rumble of tanks and amphibious craft could be heard as they made their way to makeshift concrete aprons on the sea front to be shipped to, and later from, the Continent.

Bomb damage: Cannon Street corner of Market Square

The last siren in Dover was heard on March 25. Hundreds of demob happy troops, sailors and airmen thronged the town and so a NAAFI (Navy, Army and Air Force Institute) was opened in March on a bombsite in the Market Square. It was capable of accommodating 1,500 Service men and women. The British Restaurant, which had opened during the war in the Stembrook area to enable civilians to buy a cheap, nourishing meal 'off the ration' remained and was later renamed the Civic Restaurant, causing controversy as it was seen as a public enterprise competing with commercial restaurants. Worldwide acceptance of Dover as a town of brave souls was signalled in April with the launch of an international appeal for £250,000 to

Bomb damage: Marine Station

build a Battle of Britain hospital on the white cliffs of Dover. Money quickly poured in and Princess Elizabeth (later to be Queen) agreed to be patron. This hospital was never built because the National Health Service superseded voluntary-run hospitals and the fund was wound up. Some donors claimed back their contributions, but much of the money, following a High Court hearing, was used to build the Battle of Britain homes now facing York Street.

Dover celebrated the end of the war in Europe, VE Day, on 8 May with

The Home Guard stands down at Crabble

Celebrating the end of the war from the Western Heights

bonfires and dancing in the streets. One blaze in the Market Square was fed with combustibles from war-damaged buildings and left a burned out hole in the middle of the Square. Citizens remembered the 200 or more Dovorians and about 70 servicemen and women who had been killed by the 2,226 shells, 464 bombs, three parachute mines and a trio of flying bombs that fell in the borough. The wartime services that had done sterling work, the Women's Voluntary Service, the Auxiliary Fire Service and Civil Defence, 'stood down,' but the St John Ambulance continued to provide the town's ambulance service. The Royal Victoria Hospital returned from its wartime home at Waldershare Mansion.

Field Marshal Montgomery in Dover to receive the Freedom in 1946 with Mr Renwick, Head of Dover College

The crowds were out again to celebrate V-J Day (victory in the Far East), bringing the end to six weary years of war. As well as the official celebration bonfire on Whinless Down, sea front seats were also put on unofficial bonfires. The Freedom of the Borough was offered to Field Marshal Montgomery, which he accepted in 1946.

Slowly Dover's population increased as people returned and the 2,000 empty houses were gradually reoccupied. From January to

3

Arthur Goodfellow, Mayor of Dover, with party to unveil a tablet commemorating the help of Belgian workmen rebuilding Dover

December, the population increased from 22,000 to some 30,000. During the most perilous days of war it was only about 12,000. Pre-war it had been 44,000. The increasing numbers meant there was a growing demand for homes in a town that had lost hundreds of houses during the conflict – 1869 had been damaged. Thankful Belgians repaired or rebuilt damaged houses in Barton Road, Norman and Saxon Streets and Effingham Crescent. There is still a commemorative tablet in the centre of the Barton Road terrace (numbers 61 to 75) and another in Effingham Crescent. German prisoners of war were used to repair roads and dig

Prefabs on Buckland Estate

War-damaged St Barnabas Church, demolished 1954

foundations for what was to become the 'prefab' village on the Buckland Estate. The shift of the population from the town centre to the outskirts and the villages had begun.

Several badly damaged churches had not yet been repaired: St Bartholomew's, Holy Trinity, the Congregational Church, Wesley Hall, the Salvation Army Citadel, Charlton Church, the Unitarian Church and (new) St James. Some would be demolished.

Evacuated children returned to Dover, resulting in problems as to where they could be educated. Dover Grammar School for Girls was able to reclaim its premises in Frith Road, but Dover Grammar School for Boys could not take possession of its building above Astor Avenue. The Wrens – the Royal Navy women – were not moving out. For months the boys had their lessons in the Technical Institute in Ladywell, at the School of Art in Maison Dieu Road

War-damaged Salvation Army Citadel in the High Street

and Hillersdon House in Godwyne Road. Dover College, whose premises had also been commandeered, re-opened in September.

Dover's evacuated industries such as Dover Engineering and Wiggins Teape Paper Mill also returned, but Chitty's Mill was too badly damaged to be repaired (Halfords now occupies its site).

Chitty's Mill, Charlton Green pre-war

The sea front had been largely cleared of wartime obstructions but was still closed, as was the Admiralty Pier; however, anglers were allowed on the Prince of Wales Pier and the Southern Breakwater again. There was still no civilian cross Channel ferry service.

Dover, like the rest of the country, politically swung to the left. The first Labour MP for the division was elected, whilst, following municipal elections, there was a Labour mayor, Arthur Goodfellow, and for the first time Labour controlled Dover Borough Council.

To add to the discomfort of food and fuel rationing, the temperature dropped in winter to 20 degrees below zero!

Yes, Dover and Dovorians did emerge from the war with pride, but Dover would never be quite the same again. The world was changing.

Chapter 2

LOCAL GOVERNMENT

The second half of the 20th century continued the trend of less local control of local government. Central government, meeting a growing proportion of the cost in support grants, wanted a bigger say in how the money was spent. The major change, as far as Dover was concerned, was the ending of Dover Corporation with the merging of five authorities into Dover District Council (DDC) in 1974. Dover joined Deal, Sandwich, Eastry Rural Council and Dover Rural Council to create the new local authority covering a population of just over 100,000. The Borough Council was immediately succeeded by Dover Charter Trustees with little more than a ceremonial rôle. Later, Dover was granted parish council status to become a new Dover Town Council with a town mayor.

In the immediate post-war years much of the Labour-controlled Borough Council's activities were involved with planning a new Dover out of the ruins of the old. Expectations of traffic flows dictated much of the town planning throughout the second half of the 20th century and the task was not made easier by the fact that bombing and shelling had not taken out vast areas as in some towns and cities but individual properties here and there in the area.

Sir Patrick Abercrombie's 10,000-word plan for a 'new Dover' was published in 1946. It called for the reconstruction of much of the building in the Dour valley over the next 20 years. The Borough Council sought to impose compulsory purchase orders on swathes of the town including the Charlton Green area, destined to become part of Dover's industrial zone, where 68 homes and 69 war-damaged properties were included. Many buildings, such as the Burlington Hotel, were acquired by compulsory purchase and demolished.

Labour took control of Dover Borough Council for the first time in 1945 with Mr Goodfellow the first Labour mayor. Conservatives regained control later but Labour was successful for a second time in 1957. The political pendulum continued to swing for the next 20 years.

Apart from redevelopment plans, Dover Corporation was busy once the government allowed new homes to be built for the hundreds made homeless as a result of the war. By 1948 400 new homes were being provided on the Buckland Estate to replace houses destroyed in the older parts of Dover. Acres of land and some 150 homes were purchased by the town from the Crown Commissioners in the Leyburne Road and Harold Street area. Outdated houses were torn down to make space for council-owned blocks of flats.

The future of the damaged sea front area caused great controversy. Some of the properties were saved. Dover Harbour Board (DHB) in 1951 was given permission to convert six of its houses, towards the western end of the sea front, into 16 flats. Concern centred upon the war damaged houses, between Wellesley Road and Douro Place. Many wanted them repaired and converted into flats but the majority on the borough council, later supported in 1951 by government, voted to demolish them and to build new flats on the site. Those flats were to be called The Gateway, but that was years later. In 1952, after much debate, Dover

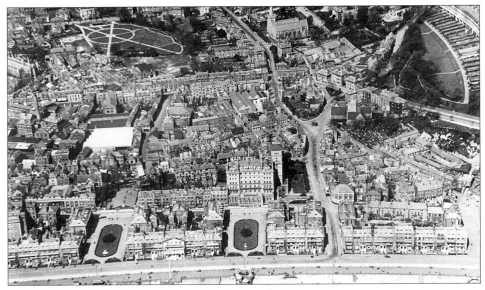

St James' area and sea front pre-war

Council published plans for 300 municipally owned high rise flats on the site at an estimated cost of £500,000. Contractors moved in to demolish scores of semi-derelict properties in Woolcomber Street, the St James' Street area and at Stembrook. Meanwhile controversy continued over the proposed high rise flats. One block was to be 15 storeys and 135 feet high, the other nine storeys. Dover Council decided that the design should be left to an international architectural

New Gateway flats with Marine Court and in the foreground the former seaplane shed/skating rink and old drill hall

competition in which more than 100 entries were received. Following comments by the Royal Fine Art Commission the Ministry of Housing demanded a reduction in the height of the two blocks of flats to ten storeys and seven, resulting in a reduction in the number of flats from 300 to 223. There were still worries about the financial implications over their construction: how much they would have to be subsidised by Dover ratepayers and how much would be contributed by the government. This delayed progress on the start of the work, but in 1956 Dover Council accepted the tender to build 221 flats at an estimated cost of just under £1,000,000. The mayor and his deputy, both Conservatives, sided with Labour to push the scheme through to end 10 years of controversy and delay. The first piles were sunk in 1957 by contractor Rush and Tompkins and in 1958 the first occupants moved in. An unplanned feature of the development occurred when green glazed tiles failed to arrive and, to avoid delay, the site engineer used instead a large number of dark green gin bottles obtained from Lukey's. They can still be seen, bottoms protruding and spaced at intervals, on the Townwall Street side of the building.

The public library

Maison Dieu House

The public library opened at Maison Dieu House in 1952. The red brick Jacobean house is probably the oldest domestic building in the town. It was built in 1665 as a residence for the Royal Navy's Agent Victualler after the conversion of the Maison Dieu into a Navy victualling store. After 1815 it became the residence for the commanding officer of the Royal Engineers in Dover until 1834 when it became a private house. Stembrook tannery owner and mayor, William

Mummery, lived there. Dover Borough Council bought it in 1904 for use as offices. Damaged during the Second World War it was converted for use as a public library.

Commercial libraries for public use started to appear in Dover in the 18th century. Apparently Mr Newport in Snargate Street boasted a stock of 7,000 books in 1769. William Batcheller built the King's Arms Library in Snargate Street in 1826 with an annual membership fee of a guinea. Andrew Carnegie, the wealthy American philanthropist, had offered Dover £10,000 for a public library, but the offer was never taken up. After the First World War, Dover's library needs were catered for by the Dover Working Men's Institute, founded in 1852, and lending libraries operated by shops such as Boots the Chemist. In 1934 Dover Borough Council bought the Institute's premises and library stock at 6 Biggin Street to form a new public library, which opened in 1935. William Munford was the first librarian, aged 23. He left Dover in 1945 and was succeeded by Bernard Corrall from 1946 until 1966. His wife, Sylvia, also worked at the library.

The Biggin Street building was destroyed in 1942, but the library reopened at 16 Effingham Crescent a fortnight later since most of the books had survived. In 1945 the library moved into the Biggin Hall with the junior library moving, in 1946, into a room under the Town Hall. Maison Dieu House became its permanent home in 1952. The Children's Library moved to new premises in Maison Dieu Gardens in 1963 and in 1968 a mobile library service commenced.

As a consequence of local government reorganisation in 1974 Dover's library became part of Kent County Library. Loaning was extended to audio cassettes, CDs and videos. By the end of the century computers including internet access was also available for public use.

During the early 1950s a car showroom, a pub called *The Roman Quay* and 34 flats were built for the Corporation in the Castle Street, Church Street, Stembrook triangle and in 1956 Dover's 1,000th post-war council house was handed over to tenants at Aycliffe.

A national development company, in 1960, bought the land behind The Gateway from Dover Corporation. Planning consent was given for a 20-storey tower of flats on stilts with shops and car parking but, as so often happened, there was a government crack down on finance and a big increase in interest rates. As a result the whole scheme was shelved and the land was sold back to the town in 1964.

Mrs Dorothy Bushell (Labour) was elected the first woman mayor of Dover in 1960. In the following year, the Conservatives were again in power after four years in opposition. Three years later the pendulum swung again with Labour dominant. In a home-building frenzy Labour vowed it would provide another 1,000 council houses and flats in the following six years of which 300 would be on grazing land opposite Archers Court School on the boundary with Whitfield. In 1968 it was announced that 2,000 new council homes had been built since the war. The mid-1960s saw a development boom when a number of older Dover properties were demolished to make way for future construction. Planning consent was given for about 100 new homes on the hills at River and 39 at Eaves Road while the first council-owned homes on the Green Lane estate were

Dorothy Bushell, first woman mayor, 1960

completed. One scheme that never made progress, revealed in 1969, was for the development of part of the Western Heights with homes, an hotel and leisure facilities. Fortunately, the plans were rejected.

In 1970 work started on the construction of Dover Council's swimming pool at the Woolcomber Street-Townwall Street junction and by 1975 a £300,000 sports centre was under construction alongside it.

Local controversies included the celebrated Cowper Road 'gate case' in which the Town Clerk, James A Johnson, was eventually ordered in 1971 to pay £100 legal costs. It was the practice at the top of Cowper Road, River, which was a dead end, for drivers of Corporation refuse collection lorries, rather than reverse all the way down, to drive through an old gateway onto private property and turn round. For some reason the owners of the property, Mr and Mrs Dixon, objected to the practice. The Town Clerk asserted that the drivers could continue because there was no gate barring entry. He lost the case.

In 1972, with Labour in control again, negotiations were in progress on the merging of Dover with other local authorities. There was plenty of political back room dealing about who should be chief executive of the new authority with Deal councillors wanting their nominee in the top job. Ian Gill, then Town Clerk of Dover, decided to take the offer of chief executive of Thanet District Council and so solicitor Ian Paterson was appointed in 1973 as Dover's chief executive, but only after John Wood apparently accepted it and then declined at the last minute.

On 1 April 1974 came the merger of the five local authorities with Conservatives in control and much rivalry between different groups as to where the headquarters should be. Labour wanted to lease the 12-storey Townwall Street office block to bring together staff scattered in 15 different offices, but the idea was rejected on cost grounds. With the merger came the unwelcome news for ratepayers of 25% to 50% rate increases.

Dover Borough's last mayor was Peter Bean (Conservative) and the first Charter Trustees town mayor was Peter Mee (Labour). Dover and Calais were officially "twinned." Dover already had links with Split in Yugoslavia.

1976 proved to be a turbulent year for Dover District Council when chief executive Ian Paterson, also the election returning officer, rejected the papers of Alec Greenway Stanley of Deal, a leading district Conservative councillor. The issue was over a hyphen in the name Greenway-Stanley. This led to rows, secret meetings, court cases and the eventual sacking of Mr Paterson. During one hectic council meeting in 1978 at Dover Town Hall a handbag was flung, resulting in another court case. Yet more trouble blew up when a senior Tory was fined £250 for failing to declare a pecuniary interest over a rating issue. He was found guilty on five of eight summonses.

Dover Charter Trustees were also in difficulties over a £36,000 loss on a Son et Lumiere production at Dover Castle, which it had underwritten.

In 1981 the District Council decided to build its central offices at Whitfield in a three-phase operation. The following year the first phase opened with the cost put at around £1 million. Work then started on the second phase costing £500,000. With the Conservatives in control the council, despite strong opposition, decided to sell council houses to sitting tenants. More than 250 were sold in a year, leaving a housing stock of around 9,000.

George Blackman, previously chief finance officer, was chief executive and in 1984, on retirement, he handed over to John Moir. Still more accommodation was needed at the Whitfield offices and so, in 1985, a third phase was started at a further cost of around £2 million. There was opposition, mostly from Conservatives, to a request by River to have its own parish council, but in 1986 River won its six year fight and River Parish Council came into being in 1987.

With the threat of the opening of the Channel Tunnel, the District Council decided to embark on a two-pronged attack to preserve jobs through tourism and industry. Tourism, because of expected speedier results, took priority and the White Cliffs Country image was adopted. Pursuing this policy the District Council took the controversial decision in 1988 to build a heritage centre on the

White Cliffs Experience (Dover Museum ref d11007)

derelict site around and over Roman and Norman remains off the Market Square at a cost of £14 million. The White Cliffs Experience, as it was called, was opened in 1991 by Princess Anne and by the year's end had attracted 200,000 visitors. Many called it Dover's white elephant but more than a million people visited it before, with mounting losses, it was closed in 2000. Another tourist attraction, the Old Town Gaol underneath the Maison Dieu, was also closed for financial reasons in the same year.

In 1992 Dover Charter Trustees applied for parish council status in order to become a town council within the Dover District. The new Town Council met for the first time in 1996.

Following a by-election in November 1993 the Conservatives lost control of the District Council for the first time since the local authority was formed in 1974. The following month an alliance between Labour, Liberal Democrats and the one Independent, Brian Walker, took control, although the Conservatives, now in opposition, remained the largest party. Labour eventually gained control by relying on the casting vote of the Labour chairman. Conservatives, one Liberal Democrat and one Independent together held the same number of seats as Labour.

Reginald Leppard died in 1994 at the age of 93. He was appointed Town Sergeant at the end of the war, serving with great dignity for 20 years. He ran the Town Hall like a military operation; everybody had to be on best behaviour inside its ancient walls! Reg, the son of a farrier, was born in Folkestone and became a fireman on South Eastern and Chatham railway trains. In 1925 he left the railway and joined his wife's family business. When war came in 1939 he joined Folkestone's ARP in the first aid team. By 1943 he was in charge of a 70-strong Civil Defence rescue team at Dover. His Town Sergeant work was recognised by his professional colleagues in 1957 when they elected him Prime Warden of the Guild of Macebearers. A religious man, he

Reg Leppard, Town Sergeant

worshipped at St Mary's Church and, as a member of Dover Operatic and Dramatic Society, took the stage in numerous rôles.

By the year 2000 one of the major local government issues was over the possible sale of the District Council's 5,403 council houses to a housing association. Labour decided not to sell. An indication of pending financial problems came from the chief executive John Moir when he warned, 'the party's over.'

Three ideas for the comprehensive redevelopment of the St James' area of Dover, known as the Dover Town Investment Zone, were put before the public at an exhibition in July 2000. Thankfully, all included the demolition of Burlington House. One was selected. A new life for the empty White Cliffs Experience was under discussion including moving in the Adult Education Centre from Westmount and the Library from Maison Dieu House plus a computer studio to create a learning 'Discovery Centre' alongside the Museum and the Bronze Age Boat Exhibition.

At the end of the century there was talk of further changes in local government, with the possibility of even bigger unitary authorities replacing district and county councils. A possible blueprint for the future was a merger with Canterbury City Council and Thanet District Council.

Characters

JAMES A JOHNSON

Dominating many aspects of life in Dover for nearly a quarter of a century was Bradford-born bachelor solicitor James A Johnson, town clerk and Her Majesty's Coroner. Utilising a brilliant brain he was feared by many, with few having the temerity to stand up to him. 'James A' was not somebody you wanted among your enemies.

He gained first-class Honours in the Law Society examinations, being placed third in the country and winning a name for himself as a determined prosecutor when he worked as deputy town clerk at South Shields.

James A. Johnson

He took up his post as town clerk of Dover in December 1944 when much of the town lay in wartime ruins, resolving to make a bright, modern town out of it. That was the sentiment of the time. Mr Johnson quickly became a controversial figure – not least when he prosecuted a much-admired leading Dover solicitor and, backed by a Labour-run town council, fought local opposition for the complete redevelopment of the centre of the town. As a result many of Dover's ancient buildings and byways, which could have been an attraction today, were lost to the demolition gangs.

Three years after his arrival he was appointed coroner and his hard-hitting investigative skills became legendary throughout the country. His painstaking probe into the *Christine* yacht affair, concerning the death at sea of 32-year-old stock car driver, Dennis Bassett, captured the national media headlines for weeks.

There were a few brave souls who stood up against Mr Johnson's domination of the town. One was Miss Pat Elnor, daughter of the Vicar of St Mary's, who was accused by Johnson of calling him a dictator. She never denied it, neither did she admit it. The town clerk issued a writ for slander – 'I always carry one in my pocket', he once joked – and demanded an apology and damages. Miss Elnor rejected his threat. Mr Johnson eventually agreed that if the lady would pay his legal costs he would forget it. She ignored him and he then offered to settle fifty-fifty on costs but again had no joy. The saga ended with Mr Johnson paying all the costs and Miss Elnor blowing the whistle on the whole affair. That result was unusual, for if you clashed with Mr Johnson you could expect trouble.

Trouble there was over the notorious 'gate' affair in Cowper Road, River, when he ordered Corporation workmen to cut down a gate that blocked a claimed right of way. The whole affair was dragged through the courts and eventually the owners of the gateway, the Dixon family, won damages in the county court where the judge was somewhat unfair with his harsh criticism of Mr Johnson and his actions.

That appeared to be the beginning of the end for James as he did not seem to regain his confidence and superiority over others in the town. What was sadly noticeable was that many of those who had deferred to Jimmy when he was dominant were willing to kick him when he was down.

There was yet another row, when the District Council removed his Registrar of the Cinque Ports nameplate from his former office at New Bridge House. Despite Mr Johnson's threats the council refused to replace it. James A, in a huff, said he would refuse to help the District organise the installation of the Queen Mother as Lord Warden of the Cinque Ports.

There was still, however, admiration in the town for much of Mr Johnson's brilliant, hard work and he was made an Honorary Freeman of Dover. He was also the last surviving Baron of the Cinque Ports, but even that rôle involved him in a controversy over the aftermath of his gift of the silver oar carried in Confederation of the Cinque Ports' processions.

He retired as town clerk in 1968, and as coroner a year later having handled 800 inquests, moving with his sister Cecile to Bournemouth but retaining business interests in the town as chairman of the White Cliffs Hotel. He died, virtually forgotten by many, with just a brief death notice in the *Daily Telegraph* and the *Dover Express* but his concealed kindness lives on through his legacy to establish the Dubris Trust, a scholarship to help Dover boys and girls to go on to further education. James A Johnson was a very strong character but also a man who, despite his bluff exterior, could be quietly kind and helpful.

Chapter 3

ROADS AND RAIL

Arguments over road access into, through and bypassing Dover lasted to the end of the century and beyond. Rail access for both locals and travellers to and from the continent continued to be abysmal, highlighted even more with the opening of the Channel Tunnel.

The 1946 Abercrombie Plan envisaged the 43 feet wide London Road becoming a 74 feet dual carriageway from Buckland Bridge to the Royal Victoria Hospital, then to the rear of the GPO and along the line of (old) York Street to a widened Snargate Street. This was to facilitate the movement of traffic to and from Marine Station and the ferries at the Western Docks. The time frame was 20 years! A series of government planning inquiries modified the sweeping changes called for in the plan, but approved a scheme for a major road to run from London Road at Buckland, through part of Cherry Tree Avenue and Balfour Road to Five Ways in Maison Dieu Road and onwards to the Eastern Docks. It was estimated 455 homes and business properties would have to go to make way for this new highway.

The first post-war road development was actually the widening of Snargate Street and the closure of Northampton Street which started in 1950 and saw the gradual closure and demolition of premises on the south side. By that time DHB had decided to concentrate its car ferry operations at the Eastern Docks. Despite local opposition, the Ministry of Transport was still insisting upon the widening of London Road at some time in the following 20 years. This caused planning blight and owners were refused permission to rebuild their war-damaged properties. Temporary premises were allowed. It was also planned to widen Folkestone Road to 70 feet and Woolcomber Street. In 1955 there was talk of Worthington Street and Priory Place becoming trunk roads. The widening of Crabble Hill was completed but the pre-war scheme to widen Buckland Bridge was not implemented. In 1956 the decision was taken to make Townwall Street and East Cliff a trunk road to the Eastern Docks.

The Minister decided in 1958 that Dover's trunk roads need not be 74 feet wide only 44 feet carriageways and 60 feet overall. There was also talk not only of widening Union Road but the railway bridge too, otherwise there would be a bottleneck – we are still waiting!

The last 'Golden Arrow' steam train 'Appledore' leaves Dover Marine, 1961

Demolition of the south side of Townwall Street in 1963 for road widening

Railway electrification reached Dover in 1959, but it was not until 1961 that steam engines ceased to pull the *Golden Arrow* boat train.

The first section of the Townwall Street dual carriageway, behind the Gateway flats, opened in 1959 and was not extended to New Bridge until 1964.

In 1964 Union Road, named after the old workhouse, which eventually became Buckland Hospital, was renamed Coombe Valley Road.

The first two traffic wardens appeared in Dover in 1966 and two years later parking meters appeared in public car parks.

At long last the widening of the single carriageway A2 between Dover and Bridge across Barham Downs began in 1967 and also from the top of Crabble Hill to Whitfield Hill. A new access road to the Western Heights destroyed part of the walled dry moat.

A town centre one-way system was introduced experimentally in 1967 and succeeded in speeding up port traffic but brought complaints from pedestrians at greater risk and shopkeepers concerned about their takings; nevertheless, following an inquiry the system was made permanent. The widening of Priory Road only created a bottleneck at its junction with Biggin Street! The demolition of buildings including St Mary's School began in 1970 in order to build the York Street dual carriageway. It was completed in 1972 after some delay to allow the excavation and preservation of important Roman remains. Having made these improvements for port traffic through the town, planning and controversy began about a new road to the Eastern Docks bypassing the town from the top of Lydden Hill through Whitfield and Guston and down the cliffs. There was talk again about widening London Road to relieve congestion or extending the one-way system from Cherry Tree to Buckland Bridge.

The A2 dual carriageway across Barham Downs was opened in 1975 but the Barham cross roads quickly became an accident black spot with 9 killed and 57 injured in the first year. Traffic lights were installed but there was a campaign for a bridge interchange, which succeeded eventually.

The opening of the Dover bypass to the Eastern Docks in 1977 made a big difference to the town's traffic; however, the viaduct over the docks called Jubilee Way was closed 20 times in its first year due to high winds. The short-sighted decision to make the bypass a single carriageway claimed 12 lives by 1981 due

Jubilee Way (A2) viaduct under construction

to accidents. A new viaduct over the railway line into what remained of the Pier District improved access to the Western Docks. In 1979 Whitfield Hill was widened.

The train night ferry sleeper service, which had started in the 1930s, ended in 1979, but the Dover-Dunkirk train ferry continued with passengers walking on board.

After much controversy over suggestions for a new A20 from Dover to link with the M20 at Folkestone the Department of Transport selected its 'preferred route' of 9km costing £24 million from Folkestone across the Alkham Valley, behind Capel, over the existing A20 to the clifftop, via Aycliffe and Snargate Street to Townwall Street. The District Council opposed the plan preferring a link to the M20 via an improved A2 and A249. Another suggestion was for a motorway underpass from Snargate Street to East Cliff. Dovorians dreaded the prospect of the town being virtually cut off from its sea front by this major route. Unfortunately, the Department had its way and dear old Dover is still suffering the consequences.

With through traffic removed from the town centre the District Council approved plans for a pedestrian precinct in Cannon Street and Biggin Street, which opened in 1981 and provoked criticism that the scheme was 'half-baked' because buses, service vehicles and 'permit' cars were allowed between the

Market Square and Pencester Road. Another problem was English daytrippers to France parking everywhere and making their way to the docks on foot. Moreover, local people were going elsewhere to shop.

Construction of the new dual carriageway A20 from Folkestone started in 1989 and was completed in 1993 to help Dover compete with the Tunnel.

In 1990 it was expected that the 7 miles of A2 from Lydden Hill to Eastern Docks would be dualled, but it didn't happen! However, the Whitfield and Eastry bypass (A256) was built by 1995.

New A20, completed 1993, cuts through Shakespeare Cliff

Dover traders were angry in 1993 about the speed of traffic in London Road after the one-way traffic scheme was extended to Buckland Bridge.

In the mid-1990s the KCC supported Impact (Improvement-Action) organisation spent £2.5 million giving a 'face lift' to parts of Dover. Snargate Street was one such area targeted. This work was complemented by refurbishment of the sea front promenade with new lawns, paving and shelters.

Dover Western Docks (Marine Station) closed 1994

1994 saw the closure of the Western Docks (former Marine) station. Although there was a suggestion to turn it into a national transport museum, work soon started on a £9 million DHB project to renovate and convert it into a cruise liner terminal.

By the end of the century the two major transport developments in recent years – the Channel Tunnel and the new A20 to the Eastern Docks – meant that trains between Dover and London took up to 20 minutes longer in order to let the international Eurostar service go through and several evenings per week Townwall Street was gridlocked by lorries queuing for the Eastern Docks. The only immediate alleviation scheme was 'Operation Stack,' which involved closing the M20 carriageway from Ashford to Folkestone and using it as a lorry queue for Dover. Continued demands to help free the town from this menace by dualling the A2 from Lydden Hill to the Eastern Docks continued to fall on deaf political ears!

Chapter 4

THE PORT AND TUNNEL

The Port of Dover is the dynamo that powers the town of Dover for many people in the area are either employed in the dock area as Dover Harbour Board (DHB), Customs or Immigration staff or on the ferries themselves. Many more service the ferry industry. Its prosperity, if not its very existence, was threatened during the half century by the possibility of a fixed link across the Channel, but by 2000 the port had weathered the storm created by the opening of the Channel Tunnel and substantial growth in cross Channel traffic meant that both the port and the tunnel authorities were planning expansion.

In 1951, for the first time, just over one million passengers crossed the Channel to and from Dover. Cars shipped numbered around 100,000. The record year of 1993, immediately before the opening of the Channel Tunnel, saw 21.4 million passengers, 3.5 million cars, 1.6 million trucks and 165,000 coaches pass through the port. By 2000 more than 16 million passengers, 2.5 million cars, 1.6 million trucks and 148,000 coaches crossed the Channel via Dover in 12 months, despite the Channel Tunnel.

Port traffic chaos in Townwall Street, 1965

The most crucial decision made by DHB in the half century under review was to concentrate ferry operations at a purpose built car ferry terminal at the Eastern Docks rather than at the Admiralty Pier in the west. This, coupled with the introduction of roll-on roll-off (ro-ro) ferries, initially designed to carry cars, and the later decision to accept freight lorries, had a direct impact on the layout of roads in Dover and that, in turn, determined the street pattern of the town. As traffic to and from the port grew so did the traffic congestion problems, despite various road improvements. By the end of the century traffic congestion on the A20 approach road was a major problem.

Although work on the construction of the £700,000 car ferry terminal, in the shadow of Langdon Cliffs, did not start until 1950, the decision to switch operations to the Admiralty Dockyard, renamed Eastern Docks, was made in 1948. The cost was then estimated at £500,000 and from then to the turn of the century around £200 million was invested in improved dock facilities to cope

Eastern Docks 1965 before the closure of Dover Industries

with the massive growth in cross-Channel traffic. Firms, such as Parker Pens, were soon relocated to make way for the ferry terminal. Many hectares of land were reclaimed from 1946 onwards, when the Royal Navy departed, until 2000.

In 1950 the railway ferries berthing at the Admiralty Pier dominated Dover's ferry scene whilst, at the Eastern Docks, Townsend Brothers were the small fry with just one ship that only operated in the summer months. Townsend's staff then numbered less than 30. Townsend Brothers bought a frigate, *HMS Halladale*,

Western Docks 1961 busy with rail freight and cargo ships in Granville Dock

'Halladale' leaving the Camber

and converted it to carry 350 passengers and 55 cars. It started service in 1950. The crew looked like naval ratings, the stewards wore white jackets and an AA man plus two nurses were also part of the complement. In 1951 *Halladale* used an unloading ramp, a converted Bailey bridge, at Calais instead of craning vehicles on and off. The first vehicle ashore was an East Kent coach. This heralded the spectacular growth of roll-on, roll-off traffic. Berths 1 and 2, purpose-built for roll-on, roll-off came into use in 1953, but were demolished later in the century, unable to cope with the larger ferries. Townsend started a freight lorry service to Calais from a ramp in the Camber at the stem of the Eastern Arm in 1958. It was a failure but a portent of things to come. The firm's growth in the following years was remarkable and the company evolved, through take-overs and mergers, into the P&O Ferries of today.

The dismantling began in 1952 of the aerial ropeway built to carry coal from Tilmanstone down to the Eastern Arm and was completed in 1955 with the demolition of the 5000 ton storage bunker. Many people will remember the Merry Dolphin in the Eastern Docks, which was a very civilised restaurant in the 1950s for passengers waiting to board.

A strange looking craft, an SRN1 hovercraft, crossed the Channel to Dover on 25 July 1959, another sign of things to come. Interestingly, that day marked the 50th anniversary of Louis Bleriot's pioneer flight across the English Channel.

The threat of a Channel Tunnel, an issue raised again by British transport minister Ernest Marples in 1964, delayed the nationalised British Rail from investing in new tonnage, but not Townsend. In 1962 the company brought into service the *Free Enterprise I*, costing £1 million, and this car ferry was followed by a series of bigger Free Enterprise vessels.

Dover's unique sea front railway closed in 1964. Laid out by the Admiralty in

The world's first manned hovercraft arrives at Dover after 123 minute crossing, 25 July 1959

1917 using materials from the cliff top railway, it carried war materials from west to east. From 1932 it was used to transport 800,000 tons of coal a year from the railhead at the Western Docks to the Eastern Arm for export. Smoke belched from the engine and coal dust went everywhere. After strong objections and petitions, coal traffic ceased. It was little used after the Second World War but sometimes a diesel engine pulled 6 trucks at a walking pace preceded by a

Sea front railway 1964

man with a red flag to warn pedestrians. On 31 December 1964 hooters sounded and workmen cheered the last load of three oil wagons and the Parker Pen wages!

Terry Sutton was on board the last trip of the ferry *Canterbury* in 1964 before it was tied up in the Wellington Dock and then towed to Belgium to be broken up. Terry remembers with some nostalgia, 'Everybody – crews and passengers – have their favourite ferries, *Canterbury* was one of mine. The huge ferries of today are nowhere near as attractive as those of yesteryear. No longer do we have the wooden decks of ferries like the *Maid of Kent*, which served Dover so well for many years, nor the *Invicta*, much-loved by its masters and crew and the travelling public. The *Canterbury* was launched in 1928 able to carry 1700 passengers, but carried only 300 first class passengers – the pride of the Southern Railway fleet. Such luxury had never been seen before on a cross Channel ferry – there was even a Palm Court. The vessel carried no cars, but became the sea link for the *Golden Arrow* train service that started in 1929. She played her part in ferrying troops and refugees during the Second World War and then resumed normal Channel duties until that last trip on the Folkestone-Boulogne run in 1964.'

The first passenger hovercraft (no cars) began operating in 1966 between Dover Eastern Docks and Calais but Townsend's company chairman, Roland Wickenden, saw no profit in that mode of transport and axed the service after the first season. However, a small hoverport was constructed at the Eastern Docks for Seaspeed (British Rail Hovercraft) at a cost of £500,000 and a single SRN4

Eastern Docks with Merry Dolphin restaurant (centre) and the portals of berths 1 and 2

car-carrying hovercraft, *The Princess Margaret*, began operating between Dover and Le Portel near Boulogne in June 1968. There were many technical problems in the first season, however. In the first 74 days 186 of the scheduled 482 flights failed to take place. Nevertheless, a second SRN4, *The Princess Anne*, joined Seaspeed's fleet in 1969. In 1976-77 a purpose built hoverport for Seaspeed was constructed at a cost of £6 million between the Prince of Wales Pier and the former North Pier, which also required the filling-in of the support structure of the Prince of Wales Pier. A bonus was the dumping of excess sand from the Goodwins, used in the construction, on to the pleasure beach.

Princess Margaret with Lord Snowdon opening the Eastern Docks Hoverport in 1968 beside a model of 'The Princess Margaret' and the real thing!

Drawbacks were the loss of the King Charles II Walk and the noise of the hovercraft for sea front residents and visitors.

The rapid increase in passengers, cars, coaches and lorries at the Eastern Docks combined with the small area of land available for parking put pressure upon Customs and Excise for ever faster

Western Docks hoverport with the unsuccessful French Sedam hovercraft on the right

Ferries moored on Christmas Day in the late 1970s

clearance to keep up with arrivals and to avoid delays. In 1971 Customs gave up confronting every passenger with 'Anything to declare' in favour of a self select system 'RED – something to declare – and GREEN – nothing to declare.' Customs clearance of imported freight was facilitated by computers from 1978, which was further improved in 1985 when the port community and Customs introduced Direct Trader Input with automatic clearance for much of the traffic.

Delays over the construction of the Channel Tunnel sparked a flurry of ferry building by both Townsend Thoresen and British Rail as well as their Sealink partners in France and Belgium. A third ferry company, P&O Normandy Ferries, joined the others at Dover in 1976 with the *Lion*, sailing on the Boulogne route. Two other ferries joined their fleet – the *Tiger* in 1978 and the *Panther* in 1980. By 1981 two jetfoils were also operating between Dover and Ostend. In 1985 Townsend Thoresen (European Ferries) took over Normandy Ferries at Dover and Portsmouth for £12.5 million. The *Lion* was sold off but *Panther* and *Tiger* continued to operate on the Boulogne run for some time. During the same year the Belgian RMT company pulled out of the Sealink consortium and signed up with Townsend Thoresen to operate on the Dover-Ostend route.

Normandy Ferries 'Lion'

Jetfoil 'Princess Clementine' in 1981

By then DHB's work force had topped 1,000. Jonathan Sloggett, DHB's Finance Director, became Managing Director in 1983, succeeding W.Taylor Allen, and remained MD until the end of the century.

The French had joined Seaspeed with their own SEDAM hovercraft but it was not reliable and in 1985 was scrapped. 1985 also brought a hovercraft tragedy. *The Princess Margaret* crashed into the Southern Breakwater of Dover Harbour with the loss of four lives.

The damaged 'Princess Margaret' 1985

The blackest day in the port's modern history came on 6 March 1987 when the *Herald of Free Enterprise*, owned by Townsend Thoresen, capsized off Zeebrugge as it sailed for Dover apparently with its loading doors still open. As a result 193 men, women and children lost their lives. Many of the crew who died came from the Dover area. Everybody knew somebody who had been bereaved and the whole town went into mourning. This led to the creation of the Dover Counselling Service to support all those affected.

'Herald of Free Enterprise'

'Herald' memorial window in St Mary's

In 1988, from February to the year's end, there was a bitter dispute between P&O European Ferries, which had taken over Townsend Thoresen, and the National Union of Seamen, resulting in ugly scenes at the dock gates and massive traffic congestion on roads leading to the docks. The cost to the employers was estimated at £25 million.

1988 P&O strike picket

Cinque Ports' Pilots

The end of an era came in 1988 when Margaret Thatcher's government decided that, with improved radar, communications and traffic control, the ships' pilots around the coast controlled by Trinity House should be disbanded and amongst these were the 86 Cinque Ports' Pilots. The event was marked by a farewell dinner in the Maison Dieu.

An informal brotherhood of Dover pilots had existed from as early as the 13th century. After a number of arguments between pilots, wardens were created in 1312 to make sure each pilot had a fair share of the work. A Fellowship of Cinque Ports' Pilots, or Lodesmen, was formed in 1515 under the control of the Lord Warden and the Court of Lodemanage. This Fellowship was officially licensed by Henry VIII in 1526 to regulate the activities of knowledgeable seamen assisting ships passing through the Dover Strait to and from the Thames and Medway. From 1616 pilots' affairs were overseen by a Jury of the Court of Lodemanage, comprised of pilots, which met at Old St James' Church. From 1689 the pilots were virtually autonomous electing four wardens from amongst themselves. Entry to the Fellowship was strictly controlled. The number of Dover pilots rose from 14 in 1526 to 56 in 1833. In 1853 the Cinque Ports' pilots were transferred to Trinity House control, although still relatively independent, and the Court of Lodemanage closed. It met for the last time in 1851 when the Duke of Wellington, Lord Warden, walked in procession in his blue coat and red collar followed by the pilots in their blue coats, gilt buttons and primrose waistcoats to old St James' Church where the court sat. Afterwards, the procession retraced its steps, as usual, to the Antwerp Hotel in the Market Square.

Each pilot had his own flag. Always self-employed, the pilots contributed to a sick pay and pension scheme, which included widows' benefit. This was important as it was a dangerous occupation. The worst tragedy occurred in 1879 when the pilots' cruising cutter was run down by a ship off Dungeness and ten of them plus most of the crew were drowned. They were constantly at sea ready for ships needing their services. A pilots' lookout house was built on Cheeseman's Head (where now the Admiralty Pier meets the shore) in 1730, which was demolished when the railway was built to make way for Town Station. A new pilot tower was constructed close to the Lord Warden Hotel overlooking Shakespeare Beach. Trains ran through an arch in it on to the Admiralty Pier, but it too was demolished in 1913 when Marine Station was built. All pilots had to be Freemen and church-

Pilot's lookout (with flag) at Cheeseman's Head, built 1730
(Dover Museum ref doo811)

Annual parade of Cinque Ports' Pilots to St Mary's Church, about 1950 (Dover Museum ref d26064)

going was compulsory. They paid for their own gallery at St Mary's with a separate entrance so that they could leave unobtrusively when needed. Until 1939 a precondition for becoming a pilot was serving a year in a square rigged sailing vessel!

Most pilots were required for war service during World War II and by 1945 there were only two left in Dover! The story is told that two pilots had to board a tug and a vessel that it was towing. They tossed a coin to decide. A bomb landed on the vessel being towed and killed everybody on board including the pilot. By 1962 there were 113 pilots wearing naval style uniform. The minimum age for entry was 35 and a Master's ticket held for at least 4 years was also required. It was still very much a club with many old traditions and with generations of pilots from the same families. The cruising cutter stationed off Dungeness always had to have 14 pilots on board, awaiting vessels coming up channel and numbers were replenished by cutter from Granville Dock including 'pyjama callouts' at night. From 1971 the pilots were based at the new Folkestone Pilot Tower, which replaced the cruising cutter. Now, with every port providing its own pilotage, this ancient fellowship, whose members were amongst the most well paid in the town, is no more.

In 1992 the following month DHB announced a £100 million redevelopment plan for the western docks to include a yacht marina, an hotel, offices, shops and a restaurant. It had the potential to create 4,500 jobs, said the port authority. Use of the inner docks by traditional cargo ships had virtually ceased with increasing use of the Eastern Arm by larger vessels. Provision of temperature controlled fruit storage facilities and new berths on the filled-in Camber at the Eastern Docks in 1992 helped make Dover the United Kingdom's third busiest fruit importing centre.

Deep sea cargo is handled in Dover by the Dover Stevedoring Company,

A busy Granville Dock

which was set up in 1946 by the George Hammond company. It began in Deal in 1767, but took over the Dover shipping agent firm of John Latham in 1875, which dated back to 1664, becoming Latham, Hammond & Company. In 1919 H A J Ryeland joined the company and six years later purchased it from partners Grant and Marsh. Son David is still in the business. The company's partners became agents for several insurance companies in the 19th century and are still agents for Lloyd's. The partners were also appointed consular representatives for many countries. In 1946 Hammond's established a deep sea pilotage service covering the Channel and the Baltic and North Seas. Today the Hammond Group, with its modern headquarters on the site of the old Oil Mills in what remains of Limekiln Street, is involved in shipping and forwarding, transport, storage, cargo handling and petrol stations.

1992 also brought fears in Dover, and nationally, of privatisation of the port. Calais was said to be interested in buying, but the threat receded when the government changed its mind. In the same year DHB bought the empty Old Park Barracks, covering 225 acres at Whitfield, for redevelopment for port related activities, calling it Port Zone. The 140 houses on the site were sold to a housing association.

In January 1993 P&O pulled out of its Dover-Boulogne ferry service and in September the same year the company decided to slim down its Dover work force of 4,000 by 450 of whom 150 were seafarers. About this time Hoverspeed laid off 40 employees, again in expectation of competition from the Channel Tunnel.

Shipping minister Lord Caithness officially opened the modernised Coastguard maritime rescue centre at Langdon Cliffs in October 1993, built on the site of the Langdon Battery.

The completion of the European Single Market on 1 January 1993, heralding the free movement of people and goods across the frontiers of Member States of the European Community, had a dramatic effect upon the activities of the port.

The new Coastguard centre on the site of Langdon Battery

No longer was there any import duty or VAT to collect at the port on EC goods carried by passengers or as freight. This meant that 85% of the freight paperwork prepared by Customs agents and checked by Customs disappeared overnight, resulting in substantial cuts in Customs and freight forwarding staff. Immigration controls remained, as did Customs controls on illegal drugs, but the old RED/GREEN system for EC travellers had to go. 'Duty frees' between Member States remained for some years as a concession to the ferry and airline operators' profits, but were finally abolished in 1999 causing a big reduction in the number of day trippers. Customs allowances for excise goods purchased in EC countries also went and travellers were allowed to bring in the much cheaper (duty paid) spirits, wine, beer and tobacco without hindrance, provided, if intercepted, Customs were satisfied that the goods were for personal use and not for resale. Despite the generous quantities that could be brought in legitimately, abuse resulted in hundreds of white vans and other vehicles making frequent trips across the Channel and Customs seizing thousands of vehicles including 40 ton lorries, tons of tobacco and many thousand gallons of alcohol all of which had to be stored and somehow destroyed. Despite additional Customs staff, by 2000 one in five cigarettes being smoked in the UK had not paid UK excise duty, with a loss to the Exchequer of billions of pounds every year.

Channel Tunnel

The long threatened Channel Tunnel finally opened in 1994, although there were teething problems and traffic build-up was slow. It was way back in 1957 that talk of a Channel Tunnel began again. The 80 years old Channel Tunnel Company's shares rose from 2/- to £1. A study group was formed and survey work, boreholes and Channel soundings undertaken. The Parliamentary Channel Tunnel Committee was revived. A tunnel came a step closer in 1964 when the British and French governments decided in principle to construct it. There was gloom in Dover but despite this DHB announced plans to reclaim another five acres of the harbour and to build two new berths. Three new car ferries were due to be in service in 1965. However, with a change of government from Conservative to

Labour the prospect of a tunnel diminished but not for long! In 1966 the prime ministers of the UK and France agreed 'in principle' that a Channel tunnel should be built and open by 1975, operated by private enterprise. The cost at the time was estimated at around £200 million. A trial tunnel was dug in 1973 2km under the sea when the construction was expected to cost £500 million and was scheduled to be finished in 1980, but the whole scheme was, however, abandoned. This was reminiscent of the earlier attempt begun in 1880 and abandoned in 1886.

The possibility of a tunnel, this time with a single-track railway, was mooted again in 1977. Six MPs, members of a Commons select committee, took evidence in Dover from local authorities and trades unions.

By 1982 several groups were preparing fixed link Channel crossing schemes ranging from bored tunnels to bridges. Not surprisingly, DHB argued against a fixed link. In 1985 the Prime Minister, Margaret Thatcher, and President Francois Mitterand reached agreement on some form of link. Eleven schemes were submitted which were quickly whittled down to a shortlist of four. Euroroute submitted a tunnel-bridge-tunnel scheme, Eurobridge a 12 lane motorway bridge and SeaContainers a twin road, twin rail tunnel. The Channel Tunnel Group's plan for a twin bored tunnel taking shuttle trains and through trains costing £2.3 billion and opening in 1993 was successful. The Channel Tunnel Treaty was signed in Lille on 20 January 1986 and was ratified in Canterbury Cathedral on 12 February. Dover's response was 'given fair competition we can beat it!' DHB decided to invest millions in improving port infrastructure.

By 1987 tunnelling work was in progress by Transmanche Link, the consortium of building contractors and the Channel Tunnel Group had renamed itself Eurotunnel. Expected costs had risen to £5.7 billion. A new access road to the works at the foot of Shakespeare Cliff was built over the hills from the Folkestone Road at Farthingloe where a temporary village for 1000 workmen was constructed. In December 1990 came the historic breakthrough when French tunnellers met English colleagues midway under the Channel making it possible for the first time in 7,000 years to

Queen Elizabeth II and President Mitterand opening the Channel Tunnel, 1994

walk from Dover to Calais. This was achieved at some human cost with eight
workers killed in accidents. Tunnelling was completed in 1991 and huge
ventilation shafts appeared at the foot of Shakespeare Cliff on the new platform
created by the tunnel spoil and later called Samphire Hoe.

When the Channel Tunnel eventually opened in 1994 at a cost of more than
£9 billion there was an immediate reduction in Dover's ferry business but the
impact was not so great as had been predicted – the Kent Impact Study of 1987
had forecast a loss of 5,000 jobs. By the end of the century, Dover Port and the
Tunnel had almost equal shares of the greatly increased cross Channel traffic.

By 1994 increasing numbers of asylum seekers and economic immigrants were
arriving at Dover including many hidden in freight lorries. This was a big problem
for the rest of the decade and beyond. The government introduced fines for lorry
drivers carrying them, the ferry operators were obliged to carry out checks prior
to loading in France and immigration controls at Dover were strengthened
considerably including the use of sniffer dogs. There were several instances of
such immigrants meeting their deaths in their attempts to evade controls, the worst
being when Customs officers found 58 Chinese dead from suffocation in a lorry
at the Eastern Docks. With tougher controls at Dover, the focus for this activity
later switched to the Channel Tunnel where desperate attempts were made nightly
to board freight trains or even walk through the Tunnel.

In 1994 the Dover-Ostend ferry link was axed and replaced by fast craft.
Western Docks Station, formerly Dover Marine, closed in the same year with the
possibility of conversion into a national transport museum. Instead, work began

Converting Western Docks (Marine) Station to cruise liner terminal

Huge cruise liners moored in the harbour are now common place

in 1995 restoring the building and converting it into an attractive cruise liner terminal. Controversial plans for a new water sports centre on the sea front beach in front of the Granville Gardens proposed by DHB attracted considerable opposition in 1994 and were rejected by the planning authority.

With Stena Line taking over from Sea Containers, which had previously bought out the British Rail ferries, the Anglo-French ferry consortium, Sealink, ended and in 1995 a new French ferry company, SeaFrance, was established and began sailing between Dover and Calais.

In that same year DHB's successful marina in the Western Docks was extended and the cruise liner terminal in the former Marine Station was officially opened in 1996. In 1998, with 140 liner calls, DHB decided to build a second terminal on the Admiralty Pier. The combined cost of the two terminals was £28 million.

Plans were announced in 1996 for a merger between competitors P&O and Stena Line to create P&O Stena with fears of 1,000 job losses. The merger was approved by the authorities in 1998, but only lasted until 2002 when P&O bought out Stena's interests and renamed the company P&O Ferries.

In 1998 DHB purchased Southern House, the former Lord Warden Hotel. It was built by the railway company in the mid-19th century and was the principal hotel for cross-Channel travellers.

1997 'Pride of Calais' able to carry 2290 passengers and 650 cars or 100 lorries – part of a P&O European Ferries 5 ship Dover–Calais service with up to 50 crossings a day

Many crowned heads and celebrities slept in the elegant bedrooms and danced in the large and lavishly decorated ballroom. Charles Dickens was a frequent visitor and Napoleon III and his wife, Eugenie, were also entertained there during a state visit. It was still a popular hotel in 1939, but then became *HMS Wasp* where naval crews were billeted

Southern House 1998

and signals rooms established. After the war, the shell-damaged building was in a poor state and was used by both British Rail and Customs and Excise as offices. Following privatisation of the railway, the building passed from one company to another until P&O Stena Line sold it to DHB for use as offices.

By 2000, traffic, especially freight, through the port was increasing again and plans were in hand to build two more ferry berths, numbered 8 and 9.

October 2000 saw the last hovercraft flights from Dover. In 32 years they had carried around 20 million passengers and cars with the loss of only four lives. Hoverspeed replaced the two hovercraft with catamarans called SeaCats.

2000 – the last hovercraft crossing

In November 2000 DHB launched an initiative to win the 'hearts and minds' and funding of various authorities over its long term proposals to expand the port possibly by constructing a huge Westport, outside the harbour along Shakespeare Beach, and to restore a rail link to the port. The people of Dover had to think hard about the loss of the beach amenity and the visual impact of such a development compared with the possible economic benefits.

Characters

RAY NORLEY

Ray Norley was a Dover right wing Tory rebel who was often in the newspaper headlines in the 60s and 70s. He did not agree with rules and regulations and believed freedom of the individual should reign supreme. It got him into lots of trouble.

Mr Norley, Dover born and bred, was educated at the old St. Bartholomew's school and served as a gunner during his National Service. He worked for a local insurance company for two years before branching out into his own business, supplying secretarial services and, in1952, began his own driving school. In the late 60s he bought a restaurant, the Topaz, in Dover High Street opposite the Town Hall.

In 1966 he joined the Conservative Party and would always be found heckling at stormy election meetings convened by his party's opponents. Whenever one of the national Labour leaders took the stage at the Town Hall, Ray would always be there in the same place, in the front row corner seat asking difficult questions. On one occasion he claimed he was issuing a writ for libel against a Labour county councillor and the then Labour agent, Ian McCartney, who later became a Labour Member of Parliament. Nothing ever happened.

Ray Norley

In time Ray was elected to Dover Borough Council and later climbed the ladder of Conservative power on Dover District Council. He fell out with Conservative colleagues on the council over the celebrated Cowper Road gate case, when he was the only Tory to vote against the leadership, and during the subsequent row resigned from the Conservative group. After the issue was fought through the courts, Mr Norley claimed he was proved right but admitted his actions had made him very unpopular.

He clashed with police and traffic wardens over parking regulations and claimed that they had a vendetta against him. He fought them in the courts, always conducting his own defence, adding to his unpopularity in some quarters.

The real trouble came when, as Tory chairman of the influential policy committee on Dover District Council, he insisted upon voting on a matter in which the Crown Court decided he had a pecuniary interest. The issue was on the possibility of 100% rating of empty property when, it was alleged (but disputed by Mr Norley) that he owned empty property in Dover High Street. Labour, jumping at the opportunity to hit out at Mr Norley, complained to Kent police, alleging he was breaking local government law. The Director of Public Prosecutions decided to take action and eight summonses were issued. Mr Norley, again conducting his own defence, pleaded not guilty at Dover magistrates' court but was convicted on five of the eight charges. He was fined £250, but did not accept that he had broken the law and appealed to the Crown Court. Still conducting his own defence – he did not have much time for lawyers – he failed and the convictions were upheld but the fines were replaced by an absolute discharge. He told the judge at Canterbury Crown Court that the whole case had been motivated by malice and political consideration. All this litigation did not go down well with the majority of his party and gradually he was squeezed out of power.

One of the biggest battles he had with fellow Conservatives was over his threat to fight a Parliamentary election against the sitting Tory MP, Peter Rees QC. This was over the UK's entry into the Common Market, described by Mr Norley as the biggest confidence trick in the history of Britain, when he threatened to stand as an anti-Common Market Conservative. Naturally this did not please his political party and the Conservatives on Kent County Council, of which he was also a member, withdrew the party whip and excluded him from their private meetings.

On one occasion he refused to pay his £155 rates on his Reading Road home in protest at what he complained was lack of co-operation by council officials in his efforts to keep down the rates. Dover magistrates issued a distress warrant after he failed to appear claiming that he had 'forgotten about the court hearing.' Half an hour later he paid the amount by cheque, believing he had made his point – and obtained publicity.

Once again Mr Norley was criticised for his rebellious attitude. He continued to express his forthright views that central and local government spending was out of control, should be slashed and made more efficient and was still condemning those in subsidised housing who could run big cars until the end, which came in 1985, when he died aged 60. How would he have coped with the tougher anti-sleaze regulations now imposed on those involved in local government? No doubt he would have rebelled.

Chapter 5

SHOPS, HOTELS AND OFFICES

There were enormous changes in shopping habits and a big reduction in the number of independent shopkeepers in Dover between 1945 and 2000. The half century saw the demise of the 'corner shop' with the trade captured by supermarkets, especially those with large out of town car parks. In 1950, surprisingly, there were still 28 bakers in Dover, 25 butchers, 39 greengrocers, 14 outfitters, 11 drapers and 19 grocers. There was just one local newspaper and Vickery's oyster bar in Townwall Street! A 1953 survey reported there were 404 shops in the immediate Dover area, employing 1,639 full time and part time staff. By the year 2000 Tesco's supermarket at Whitfield, the Co-operative Society's store at Charlton Green and Kwik Save in Stembrook were the popular stores serving Dover's food shoppers.

An early sign of Dover's renewal after the war, in July 1947, was the opening of a new hotel, *The White Cliffs*, (now *The Churchill*) on Dover sea front, by the conversion of two pre-war guest houses, the Brown House and York House.

In 1948 nurseryman G&A Clark was the first to rebuild a war-wrecked shop in Dover in Biggin Street. During the same year Boots re-opened its store in Worthington Street and others followed. Autotels converted premises at the Snargate Street-Bench Street junction to become the *Hotel de France*, later demolished in 1971 to make way for a widened Townwall Street.

Rationing, introduced during the war, was still in force in 1949 – not only certain foods, but clothing too – and it was getting worse. The sugar ration was

War-damaged Grand Hotel, Wellesley Road, prior to demolition

cut to 8 ounces a week; sweets went back on the ration at four ounces a week after everybody went mad and cleaned out the confectionery shops; milk was cut from three to two pints a week and tea was still rationed. It was not until 1954 that rationing finally ended.

A controversial decision in 1951, despite the opposition of the owner, was to demolish the badly damaged *Grand Hotel* in Wellesley Road. The owner was refused a licence to rebuild. Another sign of progress came in 1952 when work began rebuilding shops, with maisonettes above, in the Market Square between Flashman's Corner and Flying Horse Lane. Elsewhere in the town there were few signs of redevelopment.

One new trend witnessed in 1954, opposed by some members of the Chamber of Commerce, was keeping shops open at lunchtime in an attempt to boost trade. Later came calls, again opposed by some, to keep open on Wednesday afternoons, traditionally the 'early closing day'.

In 1955 work started on building shops with flats above on the west side of the Market Square, where the Carlton Club stood before the war, while a car showroom, a pub called the *Roman Quay* and 34 flats were being built for the Corporation in Stembrook. Work began in 1956 on Burton's store in the Market Square and the sorry sight of Caves Café in Bench Street was replaced with a shop and flats. In 1956 Customs and Excise moved its local headquarters into part of British Rail's Southern House (formerly the Lord Warden Hotel). With greater confidence in the town, the *Dover Stage* hotel in Camden Crescent opened in 1957 with its very modern design, built on stilts with rooms and angled balconies to catch the morning sun. Barclays Bank and the National Provincial Bank moved into their new premises in the Market Square in 1958. A change toward bigger enterprises came in 1959 when the Dover and Deal Co-operative societies amalgamated.

Dover Stage Hotel in 1987

Early in the 1960s a modern grocery shop for Lipton's opposite Hattons was opened. This later became Tesco and then Etam. To make way for the wider road to the Eastern Docks, remaining shops on the sea side of Townwall Street were demolished in 1962. Ray Warner's photographic studio was rebuilt on the other side of the road whilst the *Britannia* public house and restaurant was built next door. In the following year Orme's strange but popular bookshop in Last Lane was also demolished for York Street widening. In Pencester Road seven properties were demolished in 1964 to build a dozen shops with flats above, which were completed two years later. In the same year work was completed on new shops

Demolition of Biggin Street from Maison Dieu House to the Salutation Inn 1963

and a new *Salutation Inn* in Biggin Street, following demolition of ten old shops, from the Co-operative departmental store to the Library building. Flashman's corner of Market Square was demolished to make way for a new store with flats above. Further up the main street, in High Street, planning consent was given to build a block of 11 shops, completed in 1966, on the sites of Cunnington's and one of Turnpenny's premises.

The gradual take-over of Dover businesses by combines was reflected in 1966 by the decision of Dover Master Bakers' Association to disband. During the same year there was controversy among hoteliers and guesthouse owners resulting in a split. Founder chairman Freddie Overton was voted out of office and then set up his own group. The result was two organisations: Dover Hoteliers Association and Dover (Selected) Hotel Group. Igglesden and Graves tea shop in the Market Square closed in 1967 after 180 years.

Off Townwall Street, doubtless to the sadness of many, the St James' Street area remained virtually derelict with several acres used as a temporary car park. In 1969, however, the Royal Fine Art Commission became involved in a scheme to build a 23-storey hotel, 42,000 square feet of office space and a multi-storey car park on the land. County planners opposed the height of the planned hotel. Negotiations between the developer and the planners continued for months and it was not until May 1972 that a start was made on the £2 million construction. The hotel's height was reduced to 12 storeys, but a Swiss hotel group pulled out of the project and the hotel tower block became available for offices, although it was not used until Customs and Excise occupied five floors in 1976. The smaller building became a Holiday Inn hotel. Today the glass-fronted office block, considered by many as the biggest blot on Dover's landscape and which was never fully occupied, stands empty and forlorn with its forest of aerials its only income.

Some notable properties disappeared in 1972 including the Hotel de France and the Café de Paris in New Bridge to make way for a widened Townwall Street. In 1973 a new store for Boots the Chemist was under construction on the site of the former Baptist Salem chapel in Biggin Street and demolition was awaited of the *Queen's Head* hotel next door for inclusion in the scheme. This enabled Boots to close its store on the corner of Worthington Street as well as Timothy White's, which it had taken over, on the opposite corner. In the same year Dover's department store, Hattons in Biggin Street, closed its doors for the last time after nearly 100 years of trading. There the Misses Hatton had kept an eagle eye on their uniformed staff to ensure no flirting with customers. With drapery, fashion and furnishing departments it 'sold everything from pins to carpets.' Eddie Crush's tobacconist shop also disappeared after 30 years. After 120 years the National Westminster branch in King Street closed following a merger of the National Provincial and National Westminster banks.

Empty Burlington House in 2000

Queen's Head and Salem Baptist Church in Biggin Street, demolished 1973

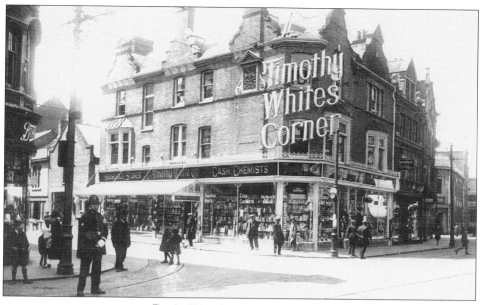

Timothy White's Corner with Boots opposite

Hattons prior to closure in 1973

All this time the potentially valuable bombsite on the acres bordered by York Street, Queen Street, New Street and the Market Square remained a blot on the town. Maybrook Properties in 1973 proposed an ambitious £5 million 'piazza' scheme for the site offering stores, shops, a covered market, offices, a museum, pub and a multi-storey car park. This caused controversy because it meant the 23 stallholders in the existing covered market, now the Dover Museum, would have to go so that the property could be demolished to allow the redevelopment. Eventually they moved into the disused Hattons store in Biggin Street. The whole project was delayed when opponents obtained a 'listing' for the facade of the former Market Hall. The only part of Maybrook's massive scheme to go ahead was the office block in York Street called Maybrook House. There were many false starts and by the mid-eighties Dover District Council admitted that the project had collapsed.

In 1975 Maples, the big furniture firm, decided to pull out of plans to open a large store in Bench Street. It was to have been the anchor tenant for the new property, built only after a controversy over the compulsory move of boot maker Fred Greenstreet from his business premises. After a short life as an indoor market the ground floor shopping area still remains empty. At this time some of Dover's shops were booming with Belgian and French daytrippers making a beeline from the port for Marks and Spencer. Morrisons, a large national chain

Crypt Restaurant in its heyday

Derelict Crypt site before fire

of newsagents and booksellers, moved into the empty Hattons premises in 1976. This later became Lavells, then John Menzies and now W H Smith.

A disastrous fire in 1977 destroyed the Crypt Restaurant in Bench Street; seven lives were lost including a fireman. The site remains empty to this day. 1977 also saw the closure of Clouts the ironmongers after 117 years in the town. Mr and Mrs Clout were popular Dovorians with their musical interests, the shop and Mrs Clout's eccentricities. Apparently she was always losing her earrings and was well known at the police station, which she visited to reclaim those found and handed in! As Mrs Clout could not cook, they always lunched out.

There was some excitement in 1979 when Miss World from Argentina visited Dover to publicise a gents' outfitters and when Gerry Stupple beat the world record for non-stop haircutting of 350 hours in his High Street salon.

Towards the end of the decade it was revealed that negotiations were in progress to persuade several shopkeepers to sell their High Street premises to a developer. Despite some planning doubts about the extent of the town's shopping zone, work began on the construction of the Charlton Centre, including a supermarket for Sainsbury's, which opened in 1980. By 1985 it was claimed that 28,000 shoppers a week were using it.

MFI opened a large DIY store in a new building on the corner of Castle Street and Maison Dieu Road in 1981. The old Dover wine merchants, John Lukey & Sons, established in 1853 in Bench Street, was taken over by the Unwins chain. There was a call for the pedestrian shopping precinct in Cannon Street and Biggin Street to revert to normal traffic because of the detrimental effect upon businesses. Hiltons shoe shop was the ninth retailer to close in the precinct but was replaced by Olivers. Others closed and were replaced: Courts furnishers in Cannon Street made way for a camping shop and Singer sewing machine premises for Contessa ladies' wear. One of Dover's best-known shopkeepers died in 1983. Henry Allison had run greengrocery shops since he was a boy. The long-established family furniture shop, Turnpenny's, closed in 1984 and was replaced by a supplier of bathroom fittings. A great loss in 1984 was the closure after 70 years of Woolworths on the corner of Priory Street with an entrance also in Worthington Street. The premises were subdivided into smaller units with W H Smith, Trueform and Mothercare opening in 1985 fronting Biggin Street. The family firms of Wakefields, gents' outfitters, and Medhurst Dairies disappeared as did the music shop Murdoch & Co., to be replaced by Our Price record shop. The popular What's New annual exhibition was held at the Town Hall for the third time in 1984 as well as a shopping week with street entertainers. Outside the town centre the Co-op closed its Elms Vale and Whitfield stores due to losses.

There were, however, some encouraging developments in the mid-eighties. W H Smith moved into larger premises in the former Hattons building when the company took over the John Menzies chain and McDonald's began trading in 1987 in the former Co-operative furniture store in Biggin Street. A stir was caused when Dover District Council suggested turning part of Pencester Gardens into a shopping complex, but fortunately it did not materialise.

The distinctive *Dover Stage Hotel* in Camden Crescent was demolished for redevelopment in 1988 but this did not happen and the site became a car park. Out of town shopping came to Dover in 1988 when Tesco closed its Cannon Street store and opened its superstore at Whitfield with 600 car spaces, creating 470 jobs and attracting 40,000 customers a week. B&Q built its large store on the site of the demolished Dover Engineering Works at Charlton Green and in the following year Texas Homecare (now Homebase) opened next door to Tesco at Whitfield amidst growing controversy that the Whitfield trading estate was sucking too much business out of the town centre. Halfords also opened a superstore at Charlton Green, where Chitty's mill once stood. A shock for Dover in 1989 was the decision by the Co-operative Society to close its extensive premises in Biggin Street and to open a £7.5 million superstore at Charlton Green next to B&Q. Its former impressive premises were demolished to make way for a modern parade of shops, which were occupied in 1994 by Argos, B-Wise and Specsavers.

In 1992 Stibbe Eurochange in Townwall Street, run by a former President of the Chamber of Commerce, was placed in the hands of a receiver and closed after a high court case when it was alleged money was owing to P&O European Ferries. Surprisingly, in 1992 Sainsbury's closed its superstore premises at the Charlton Shopping Centre in the High Street, which were occupied a year later by Premus. In 1993 DHB, the landlords of the *White Cliffs Hotel* on the sea front, refused another long term lease and the hotel closed. It reopened after refurbishment as *The Churchill*. DHB also demolished the Marine

Marine Court 1998, prior to demolition

Premier Lodge built on the Marine Court site

Court flats on the sea front to build a budget hotel, which eventually opened as *Premier Lodge* incorporating Miller's Restaurant with a controversial steel and glass round tower at one end.

The Kwik-Save supermarket opened in Stembrook in part of the old B&Q premises in 1994, but Curry's closed following a takeover by Dixons and the indoor market in Bench Street also closed. Walters, the long-established shoe shop in King Street closed during the following year as did Ludlows, the sports shop in Market Square, and Pendreich's hobby centre. In 1994 the Post Office announced that it was closing the General Post Office but post office services would be provided in the Alldays shop in Pencester Road to which there was stiff opposition, but the plan went ahead and the landmark building was demolished. Attempts were made to save its façade but Woolworths, returning to Dover after a 14 years absence, had its way and in 1999 opened a completely new building, which many consider an eyesore, with JJB Sports occupying the accommodation

General Post Office 1996 prior to demolition

Woolworths on the GPO site

above. This soon led to the closure of Dover's independent sports' shops.

A highly controversial proposal in 1995 was to open an out-of-town factory shops' complex at Whitfield. Dover traders were up in arms and the proposal went to a planning appeal and was rejected. At the inquiry it was claimed that 50 shop properties were empty in Dover. DHB revealed plans for a similar 'edge of town' factory shops' complex overlooking the Wellington Dock and this was eventually accepted. It became the highly successful De Bradelei Wharf, which

De Bradelei factory outlet beside the Wellington Dock

was soon extended. A spectacular fire destroyed the B&Q store in 1995, but it was rebuilt and reopened in the following year.

In 1998 MFI, the flatpack furniture store in Woolcomber Street, tried to relocate to Whitfield. Permission was refused so they closed down in 1999, leaving their premises empty, which were later purchased by Lidl, a French supermarket that never opened. In the same year Seeboard closed its showrooms in the Market Square leaving yet another shop empty and the gas showrooms in Biggin Street closed after 69 years in the town to be replaced by the Halifax. Another loss was Milletts in Cannon Street. Also in 1999, after much controversy, Aldi opened a discount foodstore in Cherry Tree Avenue on the site of the former Thompson's garage.

As a result of a joint KCC-Dover District Council initiative, Dover set up a town centre management, run by a public-private partnership. The first town centre manager was Kevin Gubbins, who resigned from the £20,000 a year job after only eight months in 1997 to be succeeded by Mrs Tina Pullinger, but she also departed quickly to be succeeded by Dovorian, Mike Webb, who embarked on a series of high profile schemes to attract more shoppers to the town. In 2000 a consortium of Dover businessmen launched a successful Shop Watch radio link to counter shoplifters and other criminals.

By 2000 Dover town centre still lacked large stores to attract shoppers away from Canterbury. There were many vacant premises, although there would have been several more but for the growth of charity shops. Mobile phone shops started to appear, amusement arcades were on the increase and Dover had its first sex shop.

Chapter 6

INDUSTRY

Dover's major industries returned in 1945 after the end of the war. Dover Engineering Works had been evacuated to Watford where it had helped to construct the Mulberry Harbour, which was towed across the Channel in sections, assembled and used to land men and equipment in the allied landings. On its return to Dover in 1945 the owner, Mr Elkington, was allowed to reconstruct and extend the works with a modern foundry to meet the demands of a world-wide market. Wiggins Teape returned to Buckland Paper Mill. Sadly, Chitty's Mill at Charlton Green was too badly damaged for repair and was never rebuilt. 1946 saw the start of a new gas holder to replace that destroyed in 1941 and in 1947 there were plans to enlarge Dover Gas Works to enable it to supply

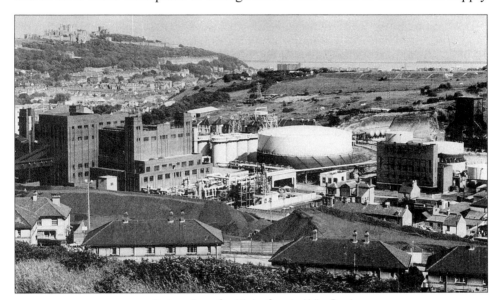

Post war Dover Gas Works, Coombe Valley Road

East Kent with four million cubic feet daily. Nationalisation followed in 1949 with plans to rebuild the gas-works completely, which began in 1952.

More businesses reopened in 1947. Kent miners celebrated the nationalisation of coal mining and the prospect of new pits opening locally. Afternoon postal deliveries disappeared leaving only two per day compared with four before the war! A new telephone exchange was opened in 1949 replacing that badly damaged in 1943.

With unemployment rising there were attempts to attract more industry to Dover. The badly damaged housing at Charlton Green (on the corner of Frith Road and Maison Dieu Road) was cleared in 1950 for a large factory intended for Portland Plastics; when it was completed, however, there were no takers until

M.O.Valve Co. opened in 1952. Kenex Coachworks moved into Castle Street to manufacture car bodies. A backward step was the closure of Leney's bottling plant in 1952. On a happier note Scott's, dyers and cleaners, celebrated 100 years with a birthday party in the Town Hall for staff.

In 1953 The London Fancy Box Co. operating in Bridge Street moved to a new factory in Beaconsfield Road and a new dairy in Crafford Street was completed for the Co-op. Dover Engineering continued to expand on the Chitty's Mill site. The Old Town Mill in Mill Lane was demolished in 1953, although it had been derelict since 1924. There had been a corn mill on the site since the 12th century, but this had been built in 1803 and milling had stopped in 1889 after which it was used as a store.

Old Town Mill demolished 1953

The reconstruction of Dover's waterworks in Connaught Road, begun before the war, was finally completed in 1955. Where Northampton Street used to run a new timber yard was provided for Tolputt & Co. with ships in the Wellington Dock able to unload timber alongside.

Dover Waterworks, Connaught Road

This was a boom time with only 126 unemployed in the area – the lowest number recorded except for the war years. The construction industry was very busy building shops, flats and schools.

Despite rising unemployment nationally with 800 locally, the highest for 20 years, there was some good news for Dover. The Engineering Works wanted to expand yet again taking over a large area including Peter Street and Spring Gardens. The Post Office took over the empty Charlton Green factory creating 50 jobs and Kenex moved to a new factory in Coombe Valley. Sadly, the old local firm of Mannerings closed its last corn mill at Buckland. In 1958 the *Dover Express* celebrated its centenary.

Proposals for a new industrial estate in Coombe Valley were scaled down because of the cost of new roads and sewers. We still suffer from the poor access to this site at the top of Coombe Valley Road.

Many of Dover's old family businesses had disappeared by 1960, but one that had survived to celebrate its centenary was Sharp and Enright, the sailmaker and ships' chandler. The business was started by a Mr Spice in 1860 of whom little is known, but it was taken over by Thomas Stanton, trading from 17 Commercial Quay with a sail loft off Blenheim Square in the Pier District. He hanged himself in about 1886 and the business was bought by Stanton's foreman sailmaker, John Enright, John Sharp and two sleeping partners connected with the George Hammond business. John Enright, a bachelor, died in 1889 and John Sharp in 1906. Sydney

Sharp and Enright

Sharp, his son, bought out the remaining partners and ran the business until the end of the Second World War when his son, John, joined the business with his son, the present owner, Michael, entering the family firm in 1955. When Dover Harbour Board demolished Commercial Quay in 1928-29, the business moved to Snargate Street, first 68A and then 133, where it is today, despite the loss of most of its former business supplying the many cargo ships that used the inner harbours. Now it relies more upon the pleasure craft of the marina. Whilst there are no sons, Michael's daughter, Sarah, looks set to carry on the business.

In 1960 the Borough Council asked the government for new heavy industry to help unemployment, but the London Fancy Box Co. was doing well trebling in size and the toy company, Gheysens, moved from the old Buckland tramsheds (now Hollis Motors) to a new factory in Lorne Road; Leney's Table Waters, however, closed after nearly 50 years as did British Rail's Priory Goods Depot. Lydden Hill Ordnance Depot was for sale. These developments were followed in 1962 by Kenex Coachworks being bought out and closing with the loss of 100 jobs. To offset this, a manufacturer of electrical measuring equipment, AVO, opened at Archcliffe on former War Office land. It expanded quickly and was worried about not having enough workers in a town with high employment!

Vivian Elkington of Dover Engineering Works died, aged 82, in 1964.

The premises of an old Dover firm in Snargate Street, Scott's the dyers and cleaners that closed in the early 1960s, were demolished in 1965 to make way for two petrol stations. The business had been started single-handed in 1852 by John Scott at 46 Snargate Street. Later he moved further up Snargate Street with a dyehouse at the rear in Northampton Street and then took over another dyer's premises in St James' Lane. In need of even larger premises Philip Stiff's former iron foundry premises in Snargate Street became available and were soon converted. The vast quantities of water required came from Scott's own well. Work came to Dover from Scott's shops and agents all over Kent and Sussex keeping a staff of around 50 more than busy.

A blaze destroyed Commercial Buildings, the former Oil Mills, in Limekiln Street in 1965. In the mid 1960s a big new factory for AVO, by then employing 800, was under construction at Archcliffe. By 1967 a new four-storey Post Office telephone exchange was under construction overlooking Maison Dieu Gardens at the back of Biggin Street.

Advertisement for Scott's Dyers and Cleaners
(Dover Museum ref d06569)

Expansion at AVO, Archcliffe

Parker Pens had been based at the Eastern Docks since 1948, but in 1968 DHB needed the space for port operations and refused to renew the lease. Consequently the firm moved out with the loss of 163 local jobs. In the same year AVO was taken over by Thorn Electricals and the Ordnance Depot at St John's Road (now occupied by Customs and Excise) closed. A number of factories

Commercial Buildings (former Oil Mills) fire 1965

opened on the slopes of the Western Heights following purchase by the Borough Council. A sewage pumping station was being built in Elizabeth Street.

In 1969 the *Dover Express* ceased printing in Dover after 110 years and its offices were moved from Snargate Street to Castle Street prior to demolition,

'Dover Express' offices, Snargate Street (second from left)

making way for the new York Street dual carriageway. 1970 saw the end of the town's own water company when it was sold to Folkestone & District Water Co. The Coombe Valley Industrial Estate was filling up with new and transferred businesses including car importers unable to use Coombe Valley Road because of the low railway bridge; their huge transporters were forced to go via Crabble Hill, Crabble Road and Hillside. This was still happening when the century ended!

In 1972 George Hammond's new offices in Limekiln Street opened on the site of the old Oil Mills. A firework display in Dover in 1973 heralded the UK's entry in the European Economic Community with the hope that a bigger domestic market would mean more jobs. This hope was shortlived, unfortunately, when the Middle East oil crisis produced economic problems worldwide including a three-day working week in Britain.

The Post Office cable depot at the Eastern Docks closed in 1973 leaving only the port operations. A technological advance came when Miss Kathleen Goodfellow, Mayor of Dover, opened the new telephone exchange enabling Dover folk to dial their own numbers rather than via an operator!

The economic situation resulted in Dover having over 1000 unemployed in 1975 – the highest in ten years. Despite this, Dover Engineering was enjoying an export boom, but there was increasing concern about pollution from its foundry. The firm celebrated 75 years in 1977 working flat out, but became a subsidiary of Newman Industries of Bristol. AVO was also doing well. Another success story was the fire escape specialist firm, Alf McKeen's Forge and Light Engineering Co. at Temple Ewell, which had started eight years previously with £90 capital and now employed 13 workers. The car firm, Martin Walter, closed its Castle Street premises in 1975 and S E Castle & Sons, scrap and waste metal merchants in Peter Street and London Road, closed after 105 years.

Dover Engineering Works and Charlton Green from Priory Hill in the 1970s

Dover District Council, which was formed in 1974 as part of local government reorganisation, bought 25 acres at Guston for light industry in 1978. Several interesting events occurred during that year. Four editions of the *Dover Express* were lost due to an industrial dispute at Hastings where the newspaper was printed; this was only the second time in 121 years that the newspaper had not appeared. A 'runaway train' hit the local headlines when a wagon load of heavy engineering equipment ran down the track 12 miles from Martin Mill passing through six level crossings, which opened automatically, and finally halting at Richborough. Les Atkinson, a local milkman, beat 5,000 other nominations to win the National Dairy Council's Milkman of the Year competition. Why was he so popular? 'I always have a smile for every customer,' he said. In 1978 South Kent Newspapers, owners of the *Dover Express*, launched a mid-week paper called the *Dover Gazette* and in the following year the first East Kent Boot Fair, attended by 15,000 people, was held at Crabble on May Bank Holiday.

Unemployment in the Dover District reached 3000 in 1980, which was the highest since the war. School leavers were hard hit. 400 jobs were lost during the year and many workers were laid off. 20 new jobs were, however, created when Foster Transformer moved into Coombe Valley. TKM Vehicle Services also moved in but only to replace BMW moving out! In 1981 Dover Engineering was having a hard time and even AVO, soon to be renamed Thorn Electrical Instruments, had to shed 130 workers. The midweek *Dover Gazette* ceased publication and Terson's auction house in Townwall Street closed and was converted into an amusement arcade – the first of many more. The government's efforts to get inflation and interest rates down failed to help local industry despite interest rates falling from 16% in 1981 to 10% by the end of 1982. Unemployment remained high, up to 13%, for the next few years, only dropping below 10% in 1987 when jobs became available on the Channel Tunnel project. Thirty industrial starter units were planned for Coombe Valley to improve matters.

The *Dover Express* was sold again in 1984 to SENEWS and moved its offices from Castle Street to High Street. In 1987 George Pepper retired as editor and was succeeded by Tony Rickson – only the eighth editor in 129 years.

David Meyer of East Kent Fairs organised the first What's New exhibition in 1986 as well as one of the brightest events of the year – the Dover Festival of Fun spread over five days.

The Channel Tunnel workings were having a considerable impact locally. In addition to complaints about noise from Aycliffe residents – three million cubic metres of marl from the tunnel were creating a huge platform, now called Samphire Hoe, at the foot of Shakespeare Cliff – a huge work camp was built at Farthingloe to house 1000 workers and a local shortage of skilled workers resulted.

In 1985 Dover Ships Stores (Flood Foods) was taken over and in 1987 the local managers of the Thorn EMI factory bought out the Dover business and named it AVO once again. Local bosses also bought out the East Kent Road Car Company.

The end of an era came in 1988 when Dover Engineering called in the receiver. The company was bought by Parkfield Group and production was moved to Coombe Valley but only 23 out of 155 jobs were saved. The Charlton Green complex was demolished and a B&Q superstore and car park was built on the site, followed later by a Co-op supermarket. The 40 acres Honeywood industrial estate at Whitfield was extended by 64 acres.

1988 also saw the launch by the Kent Messenger Group of the *Dover Mercury* weekly newspaper with the slogan, 'Giving Dover the quality newspaper it deserves'. The Chief Reporter is Graham Tutthill, a Dovorian educated at the Boys' Grammar School who began his career with the *Dover Express* but moved to the *East Kent Mercury* in 1985. He has been commended for his balanced reporting of sensitive local issues. A life-long member of London Road Methodist Church, Graham is also one of the organists. President in 1994-5 of the Old Pharosians' Association, the old boys of Dover Grammar School, he is also joint editor of its newsletter as well as being a board member of the Dover Partnership Against Crime.

Seventy jobs were lost in 1990 when marine engineers, Aldo Manta, left Dover, but 450 new jobs were expected when McLaren, the grand prix racing firm, bought Lydden race circuit for a development centre, which has yet to materialise ? much to the delight of folk in local villages who strongly opposed the development.

'Is there anybody in Dover who has not heard of Terry Sutton?' writes Derek Leach. With a round of parties and many tributes the veteran reporter, 'Mr Dover' as he is known around town, retired officially after 45 years with the Dover Express, equalling his father's 45 years, 15 of them as editor, with the same newspaper. Since his retirement Terry seems to provide just as much copy for the newspaper but as a freelance! He is still Dover correspondent for Lloyd's List – some retirement! Born in Dover, Terry attended the Boys' Grammar School, and following National Service in the 13th/18th Royal Hussars in North Africa, he joined the newspaper in 1949 as a cub reporter and then worked his way through chief reporter, news editor, deputy editor and assistant editor jobs. He was awarded the MBE for journalism in 1991. Terry reported on anything and everything including all those council meetings that were once reported fully. Cycling to St Margaret's to cover parish meetings was another joy. He also had to cover some very tragic stories, none more so than the *Herald of Free Enterprise*, when Terry came close to giving up the job he loved. However, on his retirement he said, 'I would like to do my job all over again!' Terry has seen many changes in Dover including Dover's newspaper being printed elsewhere. No longer are election results written up on the Thursday night and out on the streets by 7am the next morning! 'We used to turn advertisers away to make room for more news. Now it's sometimes the other way round,' says Terry. 'I resented having to watch some of the loveliest parts of the town destroyed in the name of progress. Some of the architecture was excellent. The place has definitely gone down hill. I used to think that I could do something about it, but I have had little success.' Despite all the changes, Terry's devotion to the town has not changed. His commitment to Dover and its people was, and still is, expressed in many practical ways. He wrote all the scripts for Ray Warner's much loved Dover films and was the narrator for some of them. The list of local organisations that Terry is or has been involved with and the offices held is endless.

The *Dover Express* seemed to attract generations of the same families and not only the Jones family who owned the newspaper for 97 years until 1968. Bob Hollingsbee, who still contributes his 'Memories' page in retirement, and his father gave 75 years service to the paper.

An exhibition to mark the centenary of one of Dover's largest employers, the London Fancy Box Company, was held at Dover Museum in 1994 and then 250 employees and their families celebrated – one year later! The firm's Beaconsfield Road premises closed in 1998 with work concentrated at Coombe Valley and the Elms Vale Laundry was destroyed by fire. Development was also underway in 1998 of a 'freight village' called Port Zone on the former Old Park Barracks site at Whitfield purchased by DHB for port related enterprises.

Pfizer, the US international pharmaceuticals company, celebrated its 150th anniversary in 1999. Pfizer Ltd., a subsidiary of the parent company, had established a manufacturing plant at Folkestone in 1952. In order to expand they then built research laboratories and a production plant on the derelict World War I Port Richborough site at Sandwich in 1954, selling its Folkestone premises in 1965. Since then the company has steadily expanded its research, development and manufacture of human and animal medicines at Sandwich and by the end of the century, with some 5,000 workers, was the largest employer in the area. Although outside Dover town, Pfizer has had a substantial impact on the whole of East Kent including Dover by creating many highly skilled jobs and by its support, through sponsorship and grants, of local organisations, and by its promotion of science in local schools.

Dover Marquee Company celebrated its centenary in 1999 but Chrysler Jeep announced it would be moving from Coombe Valley to Milton Keynes with the loss of nearly 200 jobs.

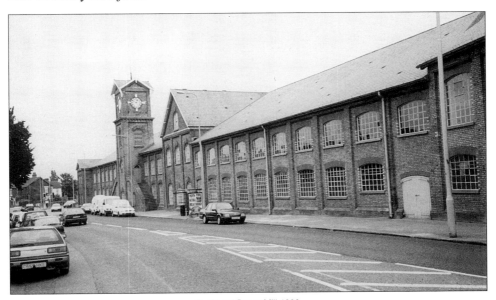

Buckland Paper Mill 1999

Another disappointment for the town occurred when hundreds of years of papermaking along the River Dour came to an end in 2000. Buckland Paper Mill, owned by Arjo-Wiggins, closed with the loss of 150 jobs and the manufacture of its world famous 'Conqueror' paper was transferred to Aberdeen. A paper mill on the site is depicted in a 1770 painting, but fire and expansion resulted in several rebuildings. Some of the present buildings, awaiting redevelopment, date from 1888. Perhaps this event sums up the 50 years – a steady reduction in Dover's old industries.

Characters

BUDGE ADAMS

To his family Budge was a hard taskmaster but to others he was a generous friend and a source of inspiration.

He was born in 1909 at 31 Castle Street. His father had established the Adams printing business in 1888 but Budge was not born with a silver spoon in his mouth. Times were hard, as they were for many in the area. Things became worse during the First World War – Budge saw the first bomb drop in 1914. His father was ill and his workers were called up – only one came back. Budge had to help in the print shop. Mother collected insurance premiums door to door. After attending a small private school Budge went to St Mary's Boys' School in Queen Street and became a Boy Scout, working in the print shop on Saturdays and in the holidays. He left school at 14 and worked fulltime in the business. His father died when Budge was 18, leaving him to run the business. He met his future wife, who was on holiday from Preston, in the Granville Gardens and married a year later, living above the shop.

Budge sailed dinghies, hiked, cycled and camped. He lived under canvas at the Warren for weeks on end but worked in the business by day! In the 1930s he cycled to Germany to see for himself what German Nationalism was all about.

When war came in 1939 Budge joined the voluntary services, servicing aircraft at Manston aerodrome until he was called up. Promoted to sergeant he was posted to Northern Ireland and the Shetlands working on flying boats before being sent to India, leaving behind a pregnant wife and two daughters. With Dover dangerous they moved to Preston. All but one of the staff in the business were called up. Budge returned home after the war, a senior Warrant Officer but a stranger to his three children, and started rebuilding the business, which thrived due to his hard work and long hours. The family home was now Waterfall Cottage in the Alkham Valley Road.

Budge was a member of the Royal Observer Corps for 26 years and was made a life member. He joined many local organisations but was never content to be just a member. In the Temple Ewell Players he was actor, producer and director; at Kearsney Bowling Club he was captain and a county coach; he was Chairman of Dover Conservatives and of St Mary's Old Boys Association; never half-hearted – it was all or nothing.

When computers came along in his 60s they became a passion and his firm was the first in Kent to make use of them. At home Budge had one computer after another as they improved.

When Budge's wife died in 1981, he retired and son Robert took over the business. Budge concentrated upon old Dover, his collection of slides and photographs and his computers. A founder member of The Dover Society when it was formed in 1988 he gave it the same energy and commitment that he gave to all his interests. He was a great campaigner as illustrated by the successful struggle to have the Charles Rolls statue moved back to its original position rather than outside the promenade toilet! Budge became very friendly with

Norwegian navy veterans from the Dover Patrol, visited them regularly and learned Norwegian.

He was fiercely independent in his later years making his own bread and wine. On his 90th birthday he received the best present he could hope for – renewal of his driving licence for another three years! He drove to William Harvey Hospital and proved that he could do 90 mph at 90 years of age – and then had his pacemaker checked!

Merril Lilley and Derek Leach with Budge Adams, aged 90, producers of 'Dover, Collected Memories of a Century'

Budge had a great love for Dover of which he had a detailed and intricate knowledge. His talks always drew a large audience. He was kind, intelligent and helpful with a sense of humour and a perfectionist. In his 90s he thoroughly enjoyed working on the book to which he contributed so much, *Dover – Collected Memories of a Century*.

He hated being ill. The day before he died in hospital he was talking about his autobiography and new projects for The Dover Society. He said that there was so much more he wanted to do that he needed to live until he was 120! Unfortunately, he didn't make it. It is left to others to ensure that his knowledge and collection of Dover slides and photographs are not lost to posterity.

Chapter 7

KENT COAL

Local jobs provided by coal mining in Kent contributed significantly to the economy of both Dover and Deal. Betteshanger, the last of the mines in Kent, closed in 1989 one year short of the centenary of Kent coal. In 1925 it was predicted that East Kent would have 18 pits employing 50,000 men. Higher wages had to be offered to attract miners to Kent. Pit villages were built at Elvington, Hersden, Aylesham and Mill Hill Deal. What began with such high expectations proved to be a long struggle with the coalfield uneconomic for much of its life due to the difficulty of extraction.

The possibility of local coal production dates back to the 1840s but investigation began in earnest when the Channel Tunnel project of that era was halted by the government in 1882 and instead the company drilled boreholes for iron and coal. In 1896 the Kent Coalfields Syndicate bought the mineral rights from the Channel Tunnel Company and built a colliery at the old tunnel workings at the foot of Shakespeare Cliff. The first coal seam was found in 1903. Over the next 25 years, mining was put in jeopardy. At least 10 collieries were started but it was 16 years before commercial coal was raised. It was very deep in thin, undulating seams. The best were over 3,000 feet (915 metres) down. There were also great pockets of water, which constantly flooded the mines. Miners had to wade in water despite pumping and some were killed in flash floods. 1000 feet deep shafts could be flooded within minutes.

By 1907 only eight tons of coal per day were being produced at the Shakespeare mine – not enough to fuel the site itself! For a brief period Leney's Brewery advertised their Dover Pale Ale as 'brewed by Kent Coal'. The pit finally closed in 1915. In 22 years it had cost £1 million and never produced commercial coal.

Arthur Burr kept the Kent mines going for almost 20 years. After the closure of Shakespeare Colliery he opened five more between 1904 and 1910 at Guilford, Maydensole, Wingham, Stonehall and Woodnesborough, but ran into similar problems. Commercial coal was eventually produced at Snowdown in 1912 and in 1913 Burr was given the Freedom of Dover; he was forced to resign in 1914, however, with allegations of being a 'conman.' He died bankrupt in 1919 with many legal actions outstanding.

Snowdown Colliery was built in 1907, closed and mothballed in 1922 and then purchased by Pearson and Dorman Long who modernised it and built houses at Aylesham for 650 families. Snowdown was the deepest and hottest and considered to be the worst pit to work in anywhere in Britain. Miners worked naked. It eventually closed in 1987.

Tilmanstone was started by Burr in 1906 and commercial production began in 1913 but the mine went into receivership in 1914. Shareholders rescued the company after Burr's resignation but it lost money every year. In 1926 it was sold to Richard Tilden Smith trading as Tilmanstone (Kent) Colliery Ltd. The pit was modernised following nationalisation in 1947 but was always uneconomic. It survived until 1986.

An unusual feature of Tilmanstone from 1930 was its overhead transport system. Having gained control of Tilmanstone Colliery, Richard Tilden Smith found the high cost of transporting the coal by rail, particularly without access to a main line, made mining uneconomic; however, he envisaged creating an overhead 'ropeway' system: a succession of buckets attached to hangers on a continuous wire, supported by 177 pylons, stretching seven and a half miles across the countryside from Tilmanstone to the Eastern Arm at Dover docks and crossing 15 roads and two railway lines. It would also be necessary to excavate twin tunnels a quarter of a mile long through the White Cliffs. On arrival at the Eastern Arm, the buckets would empty their coal into a 5,000 ton bunker to await loading on to ships. This would cost 1s 9d per ton compared with 5s 9d by

Tilmanstone Colliery in the 1980s

Aerial ropeway emerges through the cliffs on to the Eastern Arm

The Eastern Arm with its aerial ropeway and coal staithe (bunker)

conventional rail. Despite considerable opposition from the railway owners, Tilden Smith eventually obtained parliamentary approval and the completed ropeway was opened in 1930. Unfortunately, he did not live to see it operating. He died in 1929. The system was not used during the war, fell into disrepair and was dismantled in the 1950s. The demolition of the 5,000 ton bunker was completed in 1955 bringing an end to Tilden Smith's unusual enterprise.

Chislet began operations in 1913 and coal was reached in 1919. Three hundred houses were built at Hersden for its miners, many of them Welsh. Like the others, it struggled but was modernised in 1947 following nationalisation. With the end of steam trains, however, it was doomed and closed in 1969.

Betteshanger was the last to open in 1924, owned by Pearson and Dorman Long who also owned Snowdown, Wingham and Woodnesborough workings. It was the biggest mine in Kent producing coal from 1927. 1500 miners moved into the Deal area, which was resented by many locals. Betteshanger had the reputation of having the most militant miners in Kent. It was the only pit to strike during World War II when three union officials were imprisoned and 1,000 had to face a fine or hard labour, which was, however, never carried out. Betteshanger was the last to close in 1989.

Nationalisation in 1947 proved not to be Kent Coal's salvation, despite the modernisation of the pits. In 1949 the National Coal Board (NCB) invested £9 million in Kent to increase production by 50% and by 1952 production was up by 30% compared with pre-nationalisation days. Over 6,000 men were producing more than 47,000 tons per week but at a loss. Heavy losses followed in the next few years. With ample stocks of coal the NCB changed its policy of producing coal at any price. In 1959 three coalfaces at Betteshanger were closed and in 1960 there were plans to reduce manning by 1000. Betteshanger went on strike with 100 men staying underground for a week.

In 1961 miners' wages averaged £19.1s.11d. per week underground and £15.1s.4d. on the surface. By 1962 the future of the coalfield was in the balance with 6s. 4d. being lost on every ton sold. When losses were running at £1 per ton in 1964 Alfred Robens, the NCB Chairman, stated, 'Make the Kent pits pay within two years or close.' In the following year output reached a record 34 cwt. per man shift and the government's list of uneconomic pits excluded Kent. Despite this, losses continued – not helped by Richborough Power Station switching to oil in 1970; however, Lord Robens was still able to say, 'The future of Kent pits is assured due to the world shortage of coking coal.' A massive injection of money in 1973 into the industry included Kent despite continuing heavy losses. The average output per man was only half the national average due to the difficult conditions. In 1975 3,000 miners at Betteshanger, Tilmanstone and Snowdown produced one million tons of coal, which was used as coking coal for steel manufacture.

Jack Dunn, National Union of Mineworkers (NUM) area general secretary, retired in 1980 after 50 years in the industry with the coalfield producing more than ever but with little demand and stockpiles rising; the steel industry had reduced its requirements by two-thirds. In 1982 came a plan to close Snowdown for two years whilst a new rich deeper seam was investigated but with the threat of an indefinite strike a compromise was reached reducing the Snowdown workforce from 829 to 450 whilst the investigation went on.

The NCB was determined to make the industry viable by closing many uneconomic pits – threatening 2500 local jobs. As a consequence the NUM called a national strike, which lasted from March 1984 to March the following year. All three pits ceased production with a loss of £15 million to the local economy. Picketing control absorbed up to 1000 policemen with 100 arrests. Soup kitchens were set up and food and money was donated locally. A miners' wives 'back to work' campaign deplored the lack of a national ballot and the intimidation tactics of pickets, but by November only 100 men had drifted back to work in Kent. The miners lost the battle and the NCB announced plans to close Tilmanstone and then Betteshanger to which the miners responded with a big increase in output. Eight hundred jobs were lost by the end of the year, however. Snowdown finally closed in 1987 after a fight, but with investment at Betteshanger where disputes continued over the NCB's failure to reinstate 47 strikers from 1984/85. The pit continued to lose money and closed in 1989 with the loss of the last 600 miners' jobs.

Arther Scargill, National Union of Mineworkers, at Snowdown, 1973

In recent years the Kent coalfield area has attracted regeneration funding from the European Union enabling people to be retrained for new jobs in the area plus improvements to leisure and sports activities. Soon there will be little physical evidence of a century of mining, but fortunately the Coalfield Heritage Initiative was formed in 2001 to preserve and promote the heritage and culture of the Kent coalfield and its communities. An impressive sculpture, called the Waiting Miner, moved to Dover sea front when Richborough Power Station closed in 1997, is a permanent reminder of this local industry.

Waiting Miner sculpture in the Granville Gardens

Chapter 8

EDUCATION

Education in 1945 was somewhat in disarray. Schools returned from evacuation in Wales and started to rebuild themselves; although the Boys' Grammar School could not return immediately to its premises. Schools generally had to cope with increasing numbers as families returned to Dover. In addition the changes required by the 1944 Education Act were a big challenge. These included Dover losing control of elementary education to Kent Education Committee (KEC). The rather cosy set up in Dover, which had hardly changed since the 1870 Education Act, never returned. The old elementary schools with pupils up to the school leaving age of 14 had to lose their pupils at 11 years to the new secondary modern schools or the old grammar schools. In addition the post war years saw an insatiable demand for additional school and college places, which was met by enlarging existing schools and by building new ones. There was also the need to replace some. The various ambitious plans submitted by the local education authorities in Dover and Deal, however, – 21 new schools and the refurbishing of others at a cost of £750,000 – were subject to considerable delay by KEC and the government due to lack of sufficient funds.

In 1947 the minimum school leaving age was raised from 14 to 15 years, which put even more pressure on accommodation, alleviated by some temporary buildings. The new secondary modern schools, which were also co-educational, used the Barton Road and Astor Avenue schools' premises and the Castlemount buildings, formerly an expensive private preparatory school, were also adapted and opened in 1948. Shatterlocks, a new infant school in Heathfield Avenue, opened in the same year and in the following year Powell Primary School opened on the fast growing Buckland Estate.

Castlemount became a secondary modern school in 1948

In 1950 a new school in Astor Avenue was being built designed for infants and juniors, but there was local pressure for it to be used as a secondary school since two new 600 place secondary schools were considered necessary. Eventually the Minister agreed and the existing Astor Secondary School moved in 1951 leaving its old premises as a primary school. The other secondary school planned was Archer's Court costing £180,000. Cobham House in Godwyne Road, formerly a girls' youth club, was taken over by the Girls' Grammar School as an extension and Hillersdon House, used by the school for many years, was vacated.

A new Dover Technical College was planned but in the meantime expansion was needed. Westmount, a large house in Folkestone Road, was adapted for its use in 1951. It had been built as a home for Joseph Ellis, a Leicestershire colliery owner and was originally called Mount Ellis. In recent years it had housed Dover College Junior School.

Westmount, Folkestone Road

Three noteworthy retirements occurred in 1951: Mr H Jacques retired after 20 years as principal of Dover Technical College, Miss Edith Gruer retired after 23 years as headmistress of the Girls' Grammar School and Frank Holmes JP retired after 40 years at Barton Road.

St Martin's Boys' and Girls' Schools in Markland Road amalgamated in 1952 into one mixed school under Miss Clipsham, the girls' head, following the retirement of Mr Bond, the boys' head. Proposals for a new Charlton School on the Barton Road nursery site were dropped in favour of building eventually on a site at the top of Stanhope Road. This has still not happened although Charlton did get an extension in 1954!

The cost of the education service throughout Kent continued to attract much criticism and money for repairs, equipment and school transport was severely limited by the county council in 1953. The cost of school meals was increased from 7d to 9d per day. The local divisional executive considered the need for special facilities for 'backward children' such as special classes in ordinary schools for the educationally subnormal and special day schools for the more difficult cases. There were new proposals to build a Roman Catholic primary and secondary school on the site of the former Connaught Nurseries in Barton Road. Two more local school stalwarts retired in 1953: Miss Parkinson, head teacher at Barton Road for 26 years and Mr Slater, a teacher at the Boys' Grammar School since 1915. Mr Renwick, the Head of Dover College since 1934, announced that he would retire the following year.

To accommodate increasing numbers of children on the Buckland Estate it was originally planned to enlarge Powell School. Instead, a new school at Melbourne Avenue costing £12,500 for 160 infants was built and opened in 1954.

There was no technical school in Dover, but in 1954 there was an experiment at the Boys' Grammar School to enable a larger number of local boys to have a technical education. Until then some six Dover boys a year had to go to Canterbury Technical School at the age of 13. KEC wanted all secondary school education to start at 11 years of age with nobody going to Canterbury from Dover. After much local opposition, Kent relented – temporarily. The local committee wanted to keep the Canterbury facility until 25% of children could attend local grammar or technical schools, or until secondary modern schools could offer effective technical education.

The problem of large numbers of post-war children reaching secondary school age loomed with the need for more places at both grammar schools. There was space at the boys' school but little room at the girls'. Castlemount had to have additional accommodation; Barton Road was overflowing and Astor was using the Curzon Hall.

In 1955 Astor's playing fields were being laid out and the building of Archer's Court School was in progress. Only Castlemount Secondary Modern School would be left in its original buildings although there were rebuilding plans.

A new hall for the Girls' Grammar School was proposed but was cut from the Kent programme as was a new primary school for Whitfield. Accommodation at Archcliffe Infants' School was increased by using temporary huts. KEC opposed plans to build houses on the site of the demolished (new) St James' Church because it would be needed for a new St Mary's Primary School.

KEC announced that selection for grammar and technical schools would in future be based primarily upon schoolwork and head teachers' reports rather than the one-day entrance examination, which worked very well.

1956 saw the completion of the second instalment of Melbourne School and Mr A Taylor, Head of St Radigund's School, retired after serving 40 years in the area.

By 1957 Dover College was attracting scholars from many countries and a new junior school was opened at River in 1957 in a large house called Riverdale, owned earlier in the century by Willsher Mannering, the Dover miller. The junior school moved to Folkestone in 1968 and the River site was sold for housing, now called Riverdale, and the junior school eventually moved back to Dover College in 1985.

At long last the first stage of Archer's Court was brought into use in 1957.

KEC proposed that when the second stage was completed boys and girls attending Archer's Court should be separated in order to give parents in Dover the choice of a mixed or single sex secondary modern school. The local Divisional Education Executive protested but was overruled; in the following year, however, the battle was won when KEC eventually reversed its decision, enabling it to reduce by half the money needed to complete the second stage.

1958 was not a good year for the county's building programme as half of it was cut out by the Minister. The local Divisional Executive was undaunted and submitted plans to KEC to build eight new schools.

In 1959 it was announced that Aycliffe School, comprising four classrooms and a hall, would be built in 1960 at a cost of £32,000, but it was subsequently postponed; the second phase of Archer's Court costing £86,000 would be started and the Roman Catholic secondary school would be built with KEC bearing 75% of the cost.

Mr J C Booth, the Boys' Grammar School Head, retired in 1959 after 22 years and was succeeded by Dr Michael Hinton. In the same year Buckland Church of England School celebrated its centenary.

In 1960 work started on the new RC secondary school off Barton Road called St Edmund's, which opened in 1962 with Michael Mummery as the first head. It would cater for 360 children from Sandwich to Hythe. A new fee paying grammar school for St Ursula's Convent in Castle Avenue for 150 pupils opened in 1961 and was successful for a few years until a phased closure began in 1966. The premises then became St Richards RC Primary School replacing St Paul's in Maison Dieu Road. The Girls' Grammar School celebrated its Golden Jubilee in 1961 as well as the completion of its new hall. Miss Lindsay, Headmistress of Oakleigh House School, retired after 38 years. This was the last of many small private schools in Dover. Local demand for increased school accommodation was insatiable with little prospect of much progress. St Mary's School in Queen Street was standing in the way of the construction of the new trunk road (now York Street) and a new school was planned in Ashen Tree Lane; Castlemount, Astor and both grammar schools were still waiting for new or extra buildings; expanding Whitfield was still without a school with 100 children having to travel elsewhere.

KEC gave Dover good news in 1964: Castlemount would be rebuilt at long last; St Martin's primary school would be built at a cost of £68,000, St Mary's for £73,000, Whitfield for £42,000 and Aycliffe for £91,000. This allowed the old Pier Infants School to become the Harbour School for special needs with 'Jones the Harbour' in charge. Astor Secondary would be expanded at a cost of £108,000 and River enlarged for £20,000.

The future of Dover's technical college was far from certain. There was a proposal to use a retired ferry as a floating school to meet demands for more accommodation at the college. The threat of Dover losing its technical college was strongly opposed locally and eventually, in 1965, it was decided that Dover should be amalgamated with Folkestone and Ashford to form the South Kent College of Technology.

1965 brought arguments over the reform of secondary education with the Labour Government's desire for wide ability comprehensive schools to replace secondary modern and grammar schools, albeit without additional funding. The local Divisional Education Officer, Arthur Hewlett (who celebrated his 100th birthday in 2002) visited Dover Girls' Grammar School and, according to Lillian Kay the deputy head at the time, said that the Boys' Grammar would become a new sixth form college for the area and all the other schools in the area for children over 11 years would become mixed comprehensives for 11 to 16 year olds. Despite opposition from governors, teachers and parents this controversial scheme was submitted to KEC and the Ministry of Education for implementation in 1967, but was rejected and another scheme called for. The local secondary headteachers met several times to thrash out a workable scheme. They made little progress until Doctor Hinton, Headmaster of the Boys' Grammar School, eventually proposed that every child should attend a secondary modern (or comprehensive) school from 11 to 14 years and should then have the opportunity to go to grammar school with another opportunity at 16. This was submitted to the Ministry, which took a long time 'considering' before the proposal was dropped. Miss Kay was then confirmed, in 1968, as the Head of the Girls' Grammar School after being acting head for the three years of the controversy. Doctor Hinton moved away and Reg Colman succeeded him. Yet another scheme was approved by KEC in 1970 based upon two large comprehensives – one at Archer's Court and the other combining the upper Astor site and the Boys' Grammar School. A change of government from Labour to Conservative led to the scheme being dropped and the two Dover grammar schools survived.

At this time the local Council of Heads was working extremely well cooperating over selection, transport and other matters. This was well before schools started to compete with each other.

At long last the go ahead for new buildings costing £200,000 for South Kent College in Dover at the rear of Brook House was given in 1967, but was again postponed, not opening until 1972. The technical college girls based at Westmount also moved into the new buildings making way for a new adult education centre at Westmount. Whitfield had had a long wait for its school, which finally opened in 1967 catering for 320 children.

The rebuilt St. Mary's School on its new site off Ashen Tree Lane was opened by Dr Ramsey, Archbishop of Canterbury, in 1969 whilst part of Buckland School was turned into a parish centre and the remainder into a social club for Townsend Thoresen employees.

In 1970, Brian Powell, Divisional Education Officer, stated that the Boys' Grammar School buildings, dating from 1930, were no longer suitable for modern educational methods and should close within 20 or 30 years. They are still there!

An innovation in 1970 was the provision of television broadcasts on closed circuit of school programmes for local secondary schools from a studio on the Barton Road School site.

Dover College celebrated its centenary in 1971 and in the same year expelled five boys following investigations into the use of drugs. Four years later the College accepted girls for the first time.

Local schools were crowded. Astor, planned to be a new middle school, wasmoving toward 1000 pupils and extending onto Boys' Grammar School land.

Archcliffe School (Harbour) prior to demolition in 1975

Most of Castlemount was gutted by fire in 1973 but the school continued in temporary classrooms. Rebuilding was not completed until 1977.

1975 saw a good deal of school building. Harbour special needs school at Archcliffe was being replaced with a new school for 140 at Elms Vale, which opened in 1977. Vale View Primary was under construction replacing Belgrave Road Juniors. Astor Junior School was expanding prior to the closure, in 1976, of St Bart's Infants in Widred Road after 104 years.

Inflation killed the Prince of Wales Sea Training School in 1975. This merchant navy training establishment run by the British Sailors' Society off Princes Street had been in Dover since 1953. No longer would Dovorians see the

Prince of Wales Sea Training School closed in 1975

youngsters in their naval uniforms parading or climbing the mast in the forecourt; however, it was not long before the building had a new lease of life. In 1975 Dover College leased, and later bought, the premises to house its girl boarders, but vacated them in 1994 as surplus to requirements. After a few years the YMCA purchased this old building and refurbished it to provide temporary accommodation and job training opportunities for young people.

Lillian Kay, the popular Head of the Girls' Grammar School retired in 1977. After returning to her old school in 1946 as Maths Mistress, she had stayed to become Senior Maths Mistress, Deputy Head and Head for 12 years.

There was a shock in 1977 when the government announced that Nonington PE College would close in 1981. Once the stately home of the Hammond family and then a private college, it was bought by KEC and became one of the best PE colleges in Britain. Closure would mean the loss of 134 jobs – 54 staff and 80 ancillary workers.

A U-turn in 1978, however, introduced a new range of degree courses as well as classes in further education. This was not to last. In 1983 it was announced that the College would close in 1986 and this time it did. The Victorian St Alban's Court with the other college buildings and spacious grounds went on the market and are now occupied by the Bruderhof Community.

Massive cutbacks in education budgets in 1980 meant that schools had only 25% of the previous year's allocation for books, stationery and equipment; although this was later increased to 50 and then 75%. At the same time school rolls were falling by as much as 25% in some primary schools due to the drop in birthrate. Fundraising by parents helped to offset the effects of the cuts, which was praised by David Pearce, Headmaster at River and Secretary of the Dover Council of Heads. Cuts continued with KEC withdrawing travel concessions and several primary schools were ordered to close empty classrooms. Adult education fees went up by 30%.

The completion of a £1 million extension to South Kent College in 1982 meant that 460 fulltime students could be catered for by 90 staff. In the same year the Boys' Grammar School celebrated 50 years at the Astor Avenue site when the Duke of Kent attended a thanksgiving service at St Mary's followed by lunch in the school hall and a grand ball at the Town Hall.

Duke of Kent visiting the Boys' Grammar School in 1982 with Reg Colman, Headteacher, on the left and Adrian Boynton, Head of Music, on the right

Accommodation was still a problem in 1982. John Bates, Head of Archer's Court, pleaded for more classrooms to replace 14 mobiles. There were 60 mobile classrooms in use in the Dover Division at that time. Class sizes in Dover primary schools were the worst in Kent with more than 30 pupils.

South Kent College was in the news in 1983 when students designed a 'love glove' – a muff designed for the clasped hands of a loving couple. This was followed by a 'love bag'!

Anxiety about job prospects was apparently the reason for a substantial drop in pupils going on to further education in the eighties. Instead many were joining the government's new youth training scheme courses.

A national pay claim by teachers resulted in half Dover's schools closing for half days in 1984 followed by three-day strikes in 1985. The year was important for the Girls' Grammar School, which celebrated its 75th anniversary with a concert, a dinner and an exhibition of school history. Ken Farmer, Head of Astor Secondary since 1961 and Michael Mummery, Head of St Edmund's since 1962, retired in 1985.

Adrian Boynton, Head of Music at the Boys' Grammar School from the mid 70s to 1988, made a musical impression on the school – with many pupils learning instruments and making music in their own time – and on the town with excellent performances from the Boys' School orchestra, jazz band, choir and his combined Chamber Choir of the Boys' and Girls' Grammar Schools students. Admiration for his ability was only matched by the anger of parents after very

BBC Songs of Praise from Dover beach 1987 with Adrian Boynton conducting (Dover Museum ref d22948)

long rehearsals! Singing tours at home and abroad culminated in 1986 when the combined choirs and Chamber Choir sang evensong for a week at York Minister and performed in the BBC's Songs of Praise TV programme from Canterbury Cathedral. Adrian also conducted the 'congregation' for another Songs of Praise programme on Dover's beach in 1987.

That year brought a controversial plan to close Castlemount, which was suffering from falling numbers. Lillian Kay, who was then the Chairman of Castlemount Governors, led an unsuccessful campaign to save the school. Most pupils transferred to Astor when closure came in 1991, but in the meantime various grand designs came to nothing; the Boys Grammar School could move to the Castlemount buildings and Astor with 1160 pupils could take over the Boys' Grammar School site allowing Astor to be on one site (rather than both sides of

Astor Avenue). Another plan was for a sixth form centre to cater for both boys and girls from the grammar schools with the Girls' Grammar moving to Castlemount and merging with the Boys' Grammar later, since the boys' school was down to under 500 pupils and the girls' to 584 as a result of KEC policy. This idea was superseded by a suggestion for the two grammar schools to move to part of the Duke of York's Royal Military School at Guston, which also fell through. Yet another proposal came in 1992 for a combined grammar school at the empty Old Park Barracks site at Whitfield. Not to be outdone, St Edmund's also made a bid for Castlemount! The final outcome was that all the schools stayed where they were and the Castlemount site was eventually sold for housing!

Despite the absence of a comprehensive scheme, the headteachers of the Boys' Grammar, Reg Colman, and the adjacent Astor School, Ken Farmer, cooperated very well, as did the two grammar schools, moving pupils and sometimes teachers between the two buildings. Reg Colman retired in 1990 as did Elizabeth Davis, head at the Girls' Grammar. This gave KEC another opportunity to reorganise. Neither school was allowed to advertise for a new head; Neil Slater, the Boys' School deputy, was appointed for two years and Margaret Pope was made acting head at the Girls' School. Eventually the posts were filled by Mr Slater and, at the Girls' School by Dr Roger Thurling.

River Primary was extended in 1991, bringing an end to years of mobile classrooms.

In 1991 the governors of the Duke of York's Royal Military School at Guston decided to admit girls again after 150 years. The school was founded in 1801 for children of soldiers made destitute by the Napoleonic Wars and was named after Frederick, the second son of King George III who was Commander in Chief of the British Army. When it opened in Chelsea in 1803 it was called the Royal Military Asylum. Both boys and girls were admitted until 1846 when no more

Postcard of Duke of York's School

girls were accepted. The present name was adopted in 1892 and the school moved to Dover in 1909 having outgrown its Chelsea site and being in need of better facilities. The spacious new school at Guston on the Deal road looked more like a model village than a school. It had to be evacuated during both world wars, but still survives catering for the children of servicemen.

In 1993 the Boys' Grammar became a grant maintained school with far more control over its funding. At the same time Dr Thurling, Head of the Girls' Grammar, resigned on health grounds after months of controversy at the school over the handling of alleged, but unproven, sexual abuses by a teacher upon pupils.

During the 1990s a new building scheme for Astor Secondary School realised a 20 years' dream to accommodate the school on one site, allowing Astor Primary School to move into the vacated buildings in Astor Avenue in 1999 with the new name of Priory Fields. Astor Secondary's reputation for music and drama took on a new dimension when its students played the leading rôles in a production of the musical *Oliver!* in Croatia. Its new 320-seat White Cliffs Theatre opened in 1996 paving the way for the school to become Astor College for the Arts at the end of the century.

Both the Boys' and Girls' Grammar Schools were improved and extended. Elizabeth Lewis resigned in 1998 as head teacher of the Girls' Grammar to join a new trouble-shooting team being set up to help schools facing difficulties. She was succeeded by Julia Bell who is still in post.

In the nineties schools were suffering from vandalism. Arsonists caused thousands of pounds worth of damage to The Powell School in 1995. Vandals and thieves attacked the school again over the New Year, smashing 100 windows and stealing property. That same year a boy broke into Astor school, set fire to it, and then watched it burn.

On a more cheerful note Barton Junior School celebrated the school's centenary in 1998 and in the same year Astor School and Shatterlocks Infants School were both 50 years old.

At the end of the century the future of grammar schools was still in doubt with parents in the county able to vote whether to retain grammar schools or not.

Characters

LILLIAN KAY

If you belong to any organisation in Dover or you are an 'old girl' of the Girls' Grammar School, then you will know Lillian Kay. She has given hundred of talks about the Dover of her childhood since she retired 25 years ago. Lillian was born in 1914 and was brought up in the Pier District of Dover in humble circumstances. Despite one teacher considering her to be mentally retarded, Lillian obtained a scholarship to Dover's County School for Girls and thanks to a grant from Kent Education Committee studied at Bedford College for a Mathematics degree followed by post graduate training at Cambridge for a year. 'I love Mathematics,' she says, 'because of the philosophic aspects of the infinite, the marvellous intricacies of imaginary numbers and fourth dimensions and even the exact facts about the humble but fascinating triangle!' If only all teachers had her enthusiasm for the subject!

She taught at Camberley and Nottingham between 1937 and 1946 but then returned to Dover as Maths mistress at her old school, now the Girls' Grammar School. She was soon Senior Maths mistress, then Deputy Head and finally Headmistress for 12 years all at the same school.

She played hard too, running a Sea Rangers group after the war. A keen hockey player, she played for Dover Ladies and turned out as goalkeeper for the staff versus girls hockey match into her sixties. She played the violin in the school orchestra and in the Dover Orchestra and played the cello (without any instruction) in a musical trio. Fun was had at school especially with parts in the staff stage productions. A teacher's husband played God in Benjamin Britten's play, *Noyes Fludde*. He thanked Lillian by letter afterwards for allowing him to join in, 'Who else can boast of lying on the floor with the headmistress doing arithmetical progressions?' Lillian has no idea why they were on the floor!

Lillian Kay still enjoying life

Since she retired in 1977, she has kept in close touch with the school and has played a leading rôle in the Old Girls' Association and its Newsletter, taking a keen interest in former pupils all over the world – every one of whom she seems to remember! Lillian loves Dover, especially the Dover of her childhood, and, since retirement, has given pleasure to many clubs and societies talking about it. At the Old Girls' dinner in 1977, to mark her retirement, she gave a speech about the history of a very lucky person – she had always spared the school this in the past! This is how her talks to clubs and societies started. Some of the old girls present asked her to repeat her talk to various groups, which she did and continues to do, despite her 88 years.

Lillian has an enormous enthusiasm for life, which together with her sense of humour and her love for people, are still so much in evidence. 'An absorbing interest all my life has been people. I have always loved meeting people, knowing people, loving people. Life can never be boring; everyone is so different and unique. So, in a way, the unexpected development in my retirement was a very suitable one. Looking back, what a very lucky life I've had – the thirteenth child. I grew up in a world with no television, no radio, no electricity, no bath, no hot water (let alone central heating), few cars and no junk mail! When I went to college, I had no money. I'm so glad the word 'deprived' had not been invented then. It might have spoilt my illusion that I was one of the luckiest people in the world. Sometimes, I look with envy on others with children and grandchildren and even great grandchildren, but one can't have everything in life. I've had, and still have, the most wonderful friends and I live in dear old Dover, whose townspeople are so kind and ordinary.'

Lillian told her story in a highly successful book, *The Life and Times of a Dovorian* published in 1999.

Chapter 9

HEALTH AND WELFARE

From 1945 to 2000 there were probably two major concerns: the introduction of the National Health Service in 1948 and later in the century the steady downgrading of our local hospital.

In 1947 the County Hospital, formerly the Dover Infirmary and the old Workhouse, and the Royal Victoria Hospital came under a single management with interchangeable staff. When the National Health Service (NHS) took over the nation's hospitals in the following year the Royal Victoria ceased to be supported by voluntary subscription. The Hospital Workers' Fund was wound up having raised £70,000 for the hospital since 1917 and the Hospital Linen League became the Additional Comforts League. The omens were good when a new maternity block was opened at Buckland Hospital in 1949; by 1951, however, there were long waiting lists for beds.

New slipper baths were provided in the Maison Dieu Gardens in 1954 to replace those in Bridge Street sold to Dover Engineering Works to allow expansion. Free chest X-rays were available in the same year from a mobile unit, which 12,000 people attended.

Ron Proudler, a dentist, took an initiative in 1955, which led to the formation of the League of Friends of Dover Hospitals to provide comforts for patients and staff. Its first garden party raised £400 and became an annual event. Joe Harman was an original committee member and is still serving! A new recreation room for nurses was provided at Buckland.

The Old People's Welfare Service launched a meals-on-wheels service in 1956 providing meals two days per week. The Dover Moral Welfare Society opened a new hostel for girls in Folkestone Road replacing its De Burgh Hill hostel. 1956 also saw a flood of Hungarian refugees pass through Dover following the Russian invasion of their country. More than a thousand at a time were housed in local barracks and volunteers from Dover Round Table, Red Cross, St John, WVS and others helped care for them.

In 1960 there were health concerns over the discharge of raw sewage off Shakespeare Beach and calls to extend the outfall or to treat the sewage before discharge.

Modernisation of Buckland Hospital included the restoration of a two-storey block providing 60 extra beds in two wards called Ramsay and Churchill. By 1961 the hospital had 220 beds. Two new operating theatres at Buckland meant the end of operations at the Royal Victoria in 1964.

A private dwelling, 2, St Alphege Road, offered temporary accommodation for migrants for five years during the 1960s and in 1967 it became a hostel with 14 rooms for homeless women for the next 25 years. Eventually, the house and some flats in Salisbury Road were given to the Samuel Lewis Housing Trust, which were rented to the Marriage Guidance Council (Relate) for its work.

1967 brought plans for an old people's community centre behind Brook House called Riverside as well as council-run old people's homes at Whitfield,

Buckland Hospital League of Friends Garden, 1961

Aycliffe and The Glen in Folkestone Road.

The Royal Victoria Hospital was given a new lease of life in 1968 when the Countess of Guilford opened a new geriatric day unit there. Patients at Buckland benefited from the efforts of the Dover Tape Recording Society, which provided them with four hours of news, record requests, interviews and church services.

After 14 years St Monica's Church of England Girls' Home in Folkestone Road, which catered for unmarried mothers, closed. Attempts later to convert it into a community centre were refused because the Folkestone Road, which was then the A20, was considered too dangerous.

The Citizens Advice Bureau opened a Dover branch in 1971. The first health centre in Kent also opened in Maison Dieu Road. This led to a number of other purpose built group surgeries with support services and by the end of the century single doctor practices had almost disappeared.

The former home of Sir William Crundall, Woodside, at the bottom of Whitfield Hill, became a home for

Woodside 1974

'maladjusted' boys in 1974 and the Infectious Diseases Hospital in Noah's Ark Road closed but was then used as an eye unit.

A plan to improve Buckland Hospital to stand it in good stead for the next 15 years was unveiled in 1978; it included a new intensive care unit, replacement of the X-ray department, an occupational therapy unit, an extension to the orthopaedic ward, two geriatric wards, a psychiatric day hospital with Kent's first stroke rehabilitation centre at the Royal Victoria.

Brambley Hedge, a day care centre for children of single parents, opened in 1980 in the premises of the old St Bartholomew's School annexe at Tower Hamlets.

The Sisters of Charity home in Eastbrook Place celebrated its centenary in 1983. It had been an orphanage, a convalescent home for mothers and children and latterly a home for the elderly. Cairn Ryan in London Road, River was opened as a psychiatric day hospital in 1984.

The well-loved Doctor Gertrude Toland died, aged 83, in 1985. She was a Dover GP and consultant to local hospitals for 33 years including the war years.

Royal Victoria Hospital closes 1987

1987 was a sad year for Dover in more ways than one. The Royal Victoria Hospital closed after 136 years and was put up for sale at £500,000. It was bought eventually by Sanctuary Housing Association. The original mansion, built around 1834 by George Dickinson, a paper-maker, and called Brook House (not to be confused with the later Brook House built off Maison Dieu Road), was saved and converted into a hostel for the homeless but most of the remaining buildings were demolished and 44 flats built. The Victoria Hospital had opened in 1851, funded by public subscription, as a thank-offering for Dover escaping a cholera epidemic. There were just nine beds with a matron, porter and servant. Several extensions were built by the end of the century and it was named Royal Victoria in memory of Queen Victoria.

Better news in 1987 was that the £4 million facelift of Buckland Hospital had been completed; although there were signs of trouble ahead when it was described as 'only just viable'.

Dover Counselling Centre

KCC responded to the *Herald of Free Enterprise* disaster in 1987 by setting up a counselling service for all those involved. The funding was withdrawn in 1988, but the Herald Assistance Unit workers recognised the continuing needs of the bereaved, survivors and the wider community; the Dover Counselling Centre, therefore, opened as KCC withdrew, continuing to give support to those connected with the disaster but also increasing its range of counselling services to include general bereavement, addiction and marriage guidance. It continues to provide a valuable local service aided by grants from various authorities and organisations. The Herald Families Association, the group set up by those bereaved in the Zeebrugge disaster in 1987, held its final meeting in 1997, but a memorial service is still held annually for relatives.

St Martin's Emmaus

In 1994 there was need for a night shelter in Dover for the homeless, although a greater need was somewhere for them to go during the day. Francis Watts, a local Christian, was instrumental in bringing the Emmaus Movement to the town to help meet this need. Begun by Abbé Pierre in Paris in 1949 the movement with over 400 communities worldwide provides a home, work and a future for single homeless people. Every resident, or companion as each is called, must agree to

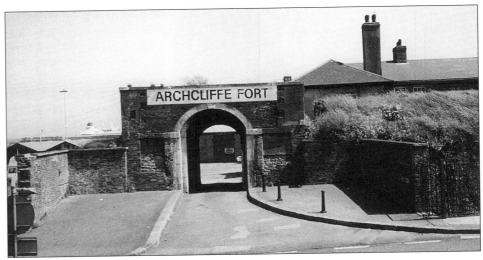

Archcliffe Fort home of St Martin's Emmaus

respect other people, to refrain from bringing alcohol or illegal drugs into the community and to be available for up to 40 hours work each week. If a room is available it is open to anyone with no questions asked. A group of people representing local churches, businesses, the District Council and St Martin's Trust, a local charity, supported the idea. The derelict Archcliffe Fort was identified as a suitable site and St Martin's Emmaus was launched in 1995. The name was chosen to link it with the local charity and St Martin, Dover's patron saint, renowned for dividing his cloak with a beggar. Kendal Beasley, a young nurse, was the first coordinator and the first 'customer' arrived on New Year's Eve. Most of the money was raised locally. The target, achieved as money became available, was to renovate buildings to house up to 21 companions each with their own en suite room and communal sitting and dining rooms plus a building to house, restore and sell donated furniture and other goods to enable the community to be self-supporting. Rosie Barnfather succeeded Kendal. By 2000 average sales were £2,000 per week. Companions sometimes just leave, but some leave to live and work locally, others stay at Emmaus for several years.

The fight for Buckland Hospital

The 1990s brought reductions in the size and facilities available at Buckland Hospital and campaigns to retain them. In 1992 a warning that a ward might close to save money led to a patients'sit-in at Dunkirk Ward. Plans to bring Buckland Hospital into the 21st century were welcomed by Cllr. Gwyn Prosser, later the local MP, but he warned that many casualty and maternity patients would still have to go to other East Kent hospitals. Services came under threat again following a decision by the Royal Colleges not to approve some hospitals as suitable training grounds for junior doctors. The Children's Ward was particularly vulnerable and a campaign to save it was launched in 1995 when the Mayors of Dover and Deal became the first people to sign the petition. It was reprieved for 18 months. Throughout 1998 there was much discussion about the future of the hospital. It was then revealed that emergency surgical services were to be switched from Buckland to the William Harvey at Ashford. As part of an overall plan, Buckland was due to have the number of beds cut from 221 to just 31. Following protests and petitions, it was decided to keep 100 beds and a minor injuries unit, staffed by nurse practitioners. In 1999 a new family birthing unit was opened.

Animal welfare

The 1990s also saw repeated, noisy and sometimes violent demonstrations outside the Eastern Docks entrance against the export of live farm animals for slaughter. By 1995 lorries carrying live sheep and calves were travelling in convoy to the docks under heavy police escort. DHB had been ordered by the High Court to accept the trade. Whilst the cross Channel ferry companies had stopped carrying the animals, farmers organised two ships for the job. The Bishop of Dover spoke out against cruelty to farm animals. Protestors were frequently arrested and nearly 100 people were fined £100 each following a sit-down protest by animal rights campaigners. It was the biggest mass arrest the town had ever seen. Police condemned protestors who dropped a lump of concrete onto a lorry carrying animals. The campaigners did have some success when a Dutch company, which carried calves for 47 hours without a proper rest, was fined nearly £10,000. Protests continued against the export of live animals and in 1999 Dover's MP, Gwyn Prosser, introduced a Private Member's Bill calling for an end to the trade, which did not, however, succeed.

Water

The 1990s brought improvements to the treatment of Dover's wastewater with the replacing of the main sewers through the town, which were laid in Victorian times, and the construction of a treatment works to replace the raw sewage outfall off Shakespeare Beach. The new plant, the size of a football pitch, was buried in a hillside near Hougham between Capel and Farthingloe.

A general shortage of water, which some thought was due to the large quantities required for the Channel Tunnel construction, led to the threat of the River Dour drying up. Millions of gallons of water were pumped into Bushy Ruff to save swans and ducks in Kearsney Abbey.

The 1990s also saw several schemes launched to help those in need. In 1996 the YMCA purchased the empty buildings of the former Prince of Wales Sea Training School in Princes Street, which had been used in recent years by Dover College to house its girl boarders. Refurbishment was helped by a £193,500 National Lottery grant. The YMCA had been active in Dover since 1856 and the new premises were intended to house homeless and jobless young people and to provide them with support and job training opportunities. In 1998 the LIFE charity opened a help line for girls and women who had unplanned pregnancies, or needed post-abortion counselling and later in the year they opened a centre. The new Buckland Community Centre was opened in 1998 on the Buckland Estate, alongside the multi-sports and play area, and various groups were quick to make use of the new building.

Asylum seekers

During the 1990s Dover had to cope with a massive influx of asylum seekers and illegal immigrants, which put welfare services under considerable strain and led to problems in the town. In 1992 the first batch of 30 Bosnian refugees arrived from former Yugoslavia and were accommodated in a youth club. By 1998 up to 1,500 immigrants were said to be living in the town whilst their appeals for political asylum were being considered by the authorities. The situation brought out the very best and the very worst in people. Representatives from local churches formed support groups, and a multi-cultural arts festival was held in Pencester Gardens, but the National Front (NF) staged a protest march in Dover against the refugees which resulted in clashes with anti-fascist demonstrators. Tensions grew amid wild claims and rumours about the favourable way the refugees were being treated. Ninety people in Westbury Road signed a petition calling for asylum seekers living next to them to be moved out and a county councillor claimed East Kent schools were refusing to take any more refugee children because they felt they could not cope. The then editor of the *Dover Express* was interviewed by police after complaints that the newspaper incited racial hatred in its coverage of asylum seeker issues, but the

Asylum seekers discovered in a lorry

editor claimed that the paper had only been reflecting the mood of people in Dover and Folkestone.

In his 1999 New Year message, the Archbishop of Canterbury, Dr George Carey, appealed to people to be more tolerant of refugees who had been forced from their homelands. 'Probably history's most famous refugee was a baby called Jesus,' he said. A week later, the NF held a protest rally in Dover, but there were more Anti-Nazi League supporters than NF marchers, and the police outnumbered both sides. The lengths to which immigrants would go were highlighted when a Kurd's bid to enter Britain illegally ended in tragedy. He was clinging to the axle under a lorry and fell beneath its wheels as the vehicle was driven off a cross-Channel ferry at Dover's Eastern Docks. As tensions grew, the government announced a scheme to disperse refugees to other parts of the country. The situation hit the national headlines one weekend in August when violence erupted in Folkestone Road and at the funfair in Pencester Gardens. Fifteen people were injured and eight, including a 13-year-old Dover girl, were taken to hospital with slash wounds. One boy's injuries required 150 stitches. An Iraqi Kurd was charged with wounding and one of the victims also appeared in court after allegedly threatening police with a knife.

Young people led the way to building bridges of friendship. Refugee and local children took part in a range of joint activities, concentrating on the things that brought them together, not what drove them apart. A number of local organisations helped asylum seekers in the town. Christians provided facilities including English lessons and a drop-in centre. Some refugees who fled the fighting in Kosovo thanked the people of Dover for their help. By the end of 1999, it was said there were fewer than 600 asylum seekers living in Dover, but there was still concern about the number of lone children arriving.

Dover Lifeboat

Tony Hawkins retired as coxswain of the Dover lifeboat in 1999 after 20 years, having been awarded the MBE in the previous year. The first Dover lifeboat, a 12 oared rowing boat manned by local volunteers, was provided by the Dover Humane Society in 1837 and it was not until 1855 that the Royal National Lifeboat Institution, founded in 1824, took over responsibility for it. A new lifeboat station was built alongside the new clock tower in 1865. The succession of rowing boats came to an end in 1919 with the first steam-powered lifeboat, *James Stevens no. 3*. Whilst it was understandable that the lifeboat station closed throughout the First World War, it was closed again in 1922 and did not reopen until 1930 when a high-speed boat, capable of 17 knots, was provided primarily to rescue aviators in the

Tony Hawkins 1998

Channel. The station was closed again in 1941 and the *Sir William Hillary* was commandeered by the Royal Navy as an air sea rescue launch. The station reopened in 1947 with *J B Proudfoot* using the MTB pens at the Camber in the Eastern Docks. John Walker was coxswain. In 1949 a new diesel powered boat was introduced, *Southern Africa*, which was replaced in 1957 by *Faithful Forester* with Arthur Lidden as coxswain. When he retired in 1979, Tony Hawkins, who had already served 16 years on the lifeboat, took over. The same year saw another new Dover boat, *Rotary Service*, with a top speed of 20 knots. At this time Dr

Dover lifeboat crew on 'Rotary Service'

Peter Welch was the lifeboat's medical adviser and went with the crew on several dangerous missions. The lifeboat berth was moved to the tug haven in the Western Docks in 1984 and in 1987 the 150th anniversary of the Dover Lifeboat was celebrated with a ball in the Town Hall. Over 600 lives had been saved. Roy Pain was honoured by the RNLI in 1991, having been Dover treasurer since 1966 (and still is) and chairman since 1982. At a cost of £1,450,000 *City of London II* arrived in 1997 full of the latest technological aids and with two 1200 bhp diesel engines. No longer are bravery and knowledge of the sea sufficient for lifeboat crews with so many gadgets to master. Dover's first female crew member was Kendal Beasley, a nurse and the first coordinator of St Martin's Emmaus, in 1996. Needless to say the camaraderie that exists amongst the crew is fantastic and is exhibited at the annual Crew Supper when legs are pulled mercilessly over incidents and gaffes in the past year. The RNLI is still supported entirely by voluntary contributions and the Dover Lifeboat Ladies' Guild works tirelessly raising funds. The lifeboat moved to a new berth on the Crosswall in 2000 when a generous legacy enabled a new boathouse to be built there.

Chapter 10

LAW AND ORDER

As in many spheres of activity local control of the imposition of justice has declined in the years since the Second World War. Perhaps that is not surprising with the increase in criminality and anti-social activity. In 1950 Dover magistrates' court only sat twice, sometimes three times, a week and it was unusual to have more than five or six cases on the court list. By 2000 Dover and East Kent Magistrates' Court was sitting four or five times a week. On occasions there were 20 or 30 cases on the lists and several courts were in session at the same time.

The greatest loss of local justice was the ending of Dover Quarter Sessions in 1971 after more than 300 years. The Recorder presided over the Quarter Sessions which sat four times a year, hence the name, with adjourned sessions when necessary also four times a year. In 1962 Robert Havers had succeeded Montague L Berryman QC. Recorder John Huxley Buzzard sat at the last Quarter Sessions at Dover. The final case to be dealt with involved an 18 years old youth who admitted stealing two pairs of sandals worth £2.50. He received a conditional discharge. Crown courts, usually sitting at Canterbury or Maidstone, took over the work.

In 1974 came the amalgamation of Dover, Deal, Sandwich and Wingham magistrates' courts with Frank Rose of Sandwich as chairman of the bench. A year later, plans for a central court complex at Dover, in Pencester Road, were revealed. It was not until 1986 that French Kier won the £2 million contract to build it with five court rooms, which opened in December 1987. The Victorian court in the Town Hall was then no longer used. Dover's County Court closed in 1996.

In the 1990s most of the cases before magistrates were heard at Folkestone, following further amalgamations. This time Dover, Folkestone and Ashford magistrates joined one

Magistrates Court, Pencester Road

bench to become Channel Magistrates. The Dover court complex became, for the most part, an administration centre but with some cases still heard there. Journalist Graham Tutthill, who covered the local courts for 25 years, remembered, 'With the merger came considerable confusion. Many cases had to be adjourned for one reason or another. Sometimes the case papers were at the wrong court, sometimes solicitors were needed in courts in different towns at the same time and on more than one occasion defendants were wrongly arrested because the records had not been updated and they were still 'wanted'. Then came the inevitable proposal to centralise the courts after it was claimed there was an 'over provision' of facilities. Despite protests and despite large sums of money having been spent on the Dover court house, most of the Dover cases were heard in Folkestone. This meant extra expense for magistrates, witnesses, solicitors, police, probation officers and, of course, the defendants, who were least able to afford it. Customs cases continued to be held at Dover, (but these too are likely to end in 2004 with plans to close and dispose of the Pencester Road building in 2009).'

The big increase in criminal work locally during the 50 years was caused primarily by the amount of smuggling through the port. In 1950, in the aftermath of the war, most contraband coming in consisted of expensive watches, jewellery and currency. The first conviction for importing illegal drugs came in the early 1960s. Later in the century drugs became the big problem as well as commercial quantities of alcohol and tobacco. In 1970 the first cases of 'people smuggling' were heard at Dover and by 2000 the growing problem of illegal immigration was impacting on the work of magistrates with a number of 'facilitators' in court for bringing people into the country.

The Home Office took possession of the Citadel on the Western Heights for use as a

Another heroin seizure by Customs, 1996

prison in 1953 and in 1957 it became a Borstal Institution, changing its name to the Young Offenders Institute later in the century. 1999 saw a serious riot at the prison, which was then converted into an Immigrant Removal Centre.

Policing in Dover changed markedly during these years. The bobby on the beat virtually disappeared as the police relied more upon cars to respond to crime, accidents and other incidents. Substantial increases in lawlessness combined with this police absence on the streets led to the proliferation of closed circuit television cameras to protect individual businesses, shopping precincts etc. With police resources stretched and targeted on serious crime, there was public concern over unchecked vandalism and antisocial behaviour by the end of the century.

A typical Customs seizure of alcohol, 1994

Characters

JOE HARMAN

Joe Harman was born in 1914 four days after the first bomb fell on Britain – in Taswell Street, Dover – and has lived all his life not only in Dover, but in the same house in St Radigund's Road. He joined Charlton Scouts in 1925 and eventually became Cub and Scout Master. His father, a police sergeant, died when Joe was only 12 years old. He went to Barton Road School and started work as soon as possible as a tram conductor to help support the family. He was one of the first to obtain a driving licence when they were introduced in 1936 and on 31 December, 1936 Joe was on the last Dover tram to move under power before taking the first East Kent bus out at 5.28 am the next morning! He graduated from conducting to bus driving and then became a bus mechanic keeping Dover's buses running throughout the Second World War as well as being in the Home Guard, having joined the Auxiliary Fire Service when it was formed in 1938.

His membership of St John Ambulance and first aid experience came in handy when Joe became an ambulance man after the war and he stayed with the service until he retired in 1978.

Joe claims to be a founder member of Dover's Hospital League of Friends dating back to 1955. Mr Proudler, a dentist, chaired the inaugural meeting, pointed at Joe and several others and said, 'You're on the committee!' and he still is. Joe organised the annual Hospital Fête for five years. He was also on the Road Safety Committee and was Road Safety Organiser. On Dover Trades Council he soon became treasurer.

Joe Harman at 87

He has attended St Mary's Church ever since meeting his wife Rosa during the war. Previously he was a member of Charlton Church.

In 1989 Joe was admitted as a Freeman of Dover. The hereditary freemanship was passed down from father to sons and to daughters for their husbands. Joe's father-in-law was a Freeman, which made Joe eligible. Unlike in days of yore, Freemen no longer receive a shilling when voting at elections, neither do they cry 'fish' on Sundays or graze their sheep on the sidewalks!

Joe has been a keen photographer since boyhood when his grandmother gave him a Box Brownie. Combined with his love of Dover and its history, this interest has meant that he has never gone anywhere without his camera – even when on duty. Consequently he has amassed a large collection of Dover photographs taken during his lifetime as well as many copies of older photographs. He was a founder member of Dover History Society in 1971 and has been its chairman for many years. Much of his spare time is spent researching different and often unusual aspects of Dover's history such as its shoemakers, its ironworks and its street lighting. Some of what he discovers finds its way into his weekly article in the *Dover Mercury* or in *Bygone Kent*. His life story and some of his research was published in 2001 by Riverdale Publications in *My Dover*. Now aged 88, he is often to be found in the Public Library poring over local records. There is little about Dover that Joe does not know and, if he doesn't know, he will soon find out.

Chapter 11

MURDERS AND MYSTERIES

What happened to little Dorothy Morris? How did raiders scale Dover cliffs to steal gold pen nibs? Who killed Valerie Osmond? These are some of the mysteries that have baffled local police since the Second World War.

In August 1950 Dorothy Rosemary Morris, aged 3, went on a Sunday school outing to Sandwich Bay. She disappeared and was never seen by her family again. Did strangers carry her away or did she die in some sort of sinking sands?

A spectacular robbery occurred in 1951 when raiders climbed down the cliffs to break into Parker Pens' factory at the Eastern Docks where they stole £20,000 worth of gold nibs for fountain pens. They then made their escape by reclimbing the cliffs.

In 1955 the body of a newborn baby was discovered stuffed in a rabbit hole at Langdon Cliffs. The inquest verdict was murder, but no one was ever arrested. During the same year an airman staged an armed siege at St Radigund's. Shots were fired and the airman was later jailed for 21 months. A terrible tragedy was discovered in Dover in December 1956 when a man murdered his wife and daughter with a pair of scissors and then hanged himself.

A soldier stationed in Dover was convicted of strangling his Dover-born wife in a local guesthouse in 1961. He received life imprisonment for manslaughter and the incident sparked off trouble between troops and local youths. During the following year a 15 year old boy was convicted of manslaughter for shooting his father at Tower Hamlets. Dover coroner, James A Johnson, held the *Christine* yacht inquest over 12 days in 1964 and sent a man for trial to the Assizes on a manslaughter charge where the prosecution offered no evidence.

The trussed up body of murdered Valerie Osmond, missing since 1968, was discovered floating in Dover's underground water reservoir at Guston in 1970. Mrs Osmond was 33 when she went missing from her Temple Ewell home and was the mother of five children. She had been knifed, her body bound by wire to a concrete post and sunk in the town's water supply. The wire had rusted through and her body came to the surface two years later. Police interviewed two men at length but no one was ever charged or arrested. Terry Sutton, who as a journalist covered the investigation, says, 'I believe I know who murdered Valerie. I occasionally see the person walking the streets of Dover.'

Temple Ewell was the scene of a tragedy in 1974 when a man killed his wife and their sons aged twelve and eight before committing suicide. In 1979 a Dover man was found guilty of murdering his wife at their Folkestone Road home and was jailed for life. In the same year a Dover mother was acquitted at Lewes Crown Court of murdering her husband at the *Diamond Hotel* in Dover.

A London court in 1981 jailed a Capel youth for five years for firing blanks in The Mall during the Queen's procession. The next year saw a daring theft from Dover Castle when raiders scaled the walls and stole £5,500 from a safe. In 1984 a Dover man was jailed for life for murdering his wife at their home in Old Folkestone Road. The *Dover Express* and a television programme threw doubt on his guilt. Was he covering for someone? Or was someone else responsible? Following an armed siege in 1987, at Gunn's the jewellers shop in Worthington Street, the business closed down after 70 years trading.

In 1988 at the Old Bailey a former Dover College pupil was jailed for an indefinite period for murdering a former college friend who allegedly raped his girl friend. Unfortunately, murder and serious assault were happening far too frequently by the end of the century.

Chapter 12

HERITAGE

In 1949 the names of the dead of the Second World War were added to the town's impressive First World War Memorial outside the Maison Dieu House Library and to the Dover Patrol Memorial. The Freedom of the Borough, which had been offered to Winston Churchill, the wartime prime minister, in 1943, was at last bestowed on him in 1951.

1951, Sir Winston Churchill in Dover to receive the Freedom

The Mayor of Dover, Councillor Reginald Snelgrove, attended the 1953 Queen's Coronation ceremony as did the Town Clerk, James Johnson, in his rôle as Joint Solicitor to the Cinque Ports. The Cinque Port Barons exercised their ancient right of attending the ceremony, but no longer carried a canopy over the sovereign. Councillor Bill Fish was Dover's Baron. In a colourful ceremony in the same year the ancient Courts of Brotherhood and Guestling met for the first time for 16 years in Dover. The Corporation held a civic lunch for 47 hereditary and honorary Freemen in the Maison Dieu.

The front page of the 'Dover Express' when news replaced adverts for the first time - Coronation June 1953

Dover Castle

The army garrison vacated Dover Castle in 1958 and in 1962 it was handed over to the Ministry of Works to preserve as an ancient monument retaining only Constable's Tower as the official residence of the local commander, who is also Deputy Constable of the Castle (the Lord Warden of the Cinque Ports being the Constable), and St Mary in Castro as the garrison church. For over 2,000 years from the Iron Age to the Atomic Age fortifications on this site had watched over and protected the gateway to England, evolving to meet the changing demands of warfare.

In 1958 the Castle took on a new rôle when underground tunnels in the cliff were adapted as a Regional Seat of Government (RSG) to control whatever remained of Kent, Surrey and Sussex after any nuclear attack. These tunnels and

Dover Castle from the north

caverns were a mixture of the old Napoleonic ones built as underground barracks for 2,000 men, known as Casemate, and those constructed during the Second World War – an underground hospital in 1941 above the old tunnels, known as Annexe, and another layer, code-named Dumpy, below the old tunnels in 1943, all linked to form a Combined Services HQ. They were adapted to cope with nuclear contamination and to provide radiation-proof living quarters for 420 people who might have to remain underground for weeks. The complex was a closely guarded secret until 1984 when it was closed.

Following the departure of the army, the Ministry of Works was left with many neglected buildings. A substantial number were demolished, including a Napoleonic powder house that the army had used as a bathhouse, the old infirmary, four barrack blocks, the drill hall, company offices and stables, the hospital block near the cliff edge and married quarters. Those remaining were all reroofed, although many remain derelict, including the magnificent Victorian Officers' Mess.

English Heritage took over the Castle in the 1980s with emphasis upon marketing it as a tourist attraction in order to generate income. Free entry ended, angering many local people particularly those who frequently walked around the Castle grounds. Tempers also rose when English Heritage decided to fell the trees on the slopes surrounding the Castle to improve the view of the curtain walls, to stabilise the slopes, restoring them as they would have been in medieval times, treeless. People soon grew accustomed to the new aspect and appreciated the glorious sight of the Castle floodlit at night.

Marketing efforts were attracting 300,000 visitors a year by 2000. As well as making the Castle itself more attractive to visitors, permanent and temporary historical exhibitions were introduced with regular open-air re-enactment events. Visitor numbers soared when the first phase of Hellfire Corner was opened to the public: namely Admiralty Casemate, which was the operations centre from which Vice Admiral Ramsay masterminded the Dunkirk evacuation in 1940. Later, in 1995 Annexe Level was opened, containing the wartime hospital and dormitories. Only Dumpy level, the RSG combined operations centre, remains hidden from public gaze.

Admiral Ramsay statue unveiled by the Duke of Edinburgh 2000

In the 1990s there was talk of a Millennium project to link Dover with its castle by cable car, but it came to nothing.

A successful project was to erect a statue of Admiral Ramsay above his underground HQ, looking toward France as he had done during Britain's darkest days of World War II. It was unveiled by the Duke of Edinburgh in 2000. Sir Bertram Ramsay had served in the Dover Patrol during the First World War and was recalled in 1939 at the age of 56 as Vice Admiral Dover, masterminding the evacuation of Dunkirk. In 1944 he commanded Operation Neptune, the Normandy landings. Tragically, he died in 1945.

Western Heights fortifications

The history of the incredible fortifications on the Western Heights has been mainly a story of demolition and neglect since 1945. First fortified in 'modern' times in 1779, the threat of invasion by Napoleon produced ambitious plans to make them the largest and strongest in the country and to house an army, not to repel an attack from the sea, but as a base to attack a foreign army after it had landed further along the coast. Between 1803 and 1814 the Grand Shaft barracks housing 1200 men were built including the remarkable three spiral staircases each of 140 steps connecting the barracks to Snargate Street. The Drop Redoubt, parts of the Citadel and the connecting lines (dry moats) between them were also built. Following peace in 1814 no further work was done until the country was threatened by Napoleon III when work continued in 1859. Four miles of protective lines were completed and the Western Outworks, South Front Barracks and Officers' Mess built. The top of the hill was also removed to give the Citadel a clear view of the Redoubt. This fortress was abandoned in 1920 but was refortified during the Second World War.

The Army remained in nominal control after the war but in 1954 the Citadel and Outworks were taken over by the Home Office for use as a prison. Whilst the property was maintained there were also insensitive demolitions, additions and alterations including the filling-in of the Western Outworks in 1959. In the same year the War Department demolished the South Front Barracks prior to handing over the area to the Dover Corporation, which had plans to use the four miles of moats as a rubbish tip! Fortunately, John Peverley initiated a successful campaign to protect the fortifications by scheduling them as an Ancient Monument in 1962. However, this did not prevent the demolition in the 1960s of Archcliffe Gate and part of the adjoining lines on the seaward side. The creation of a new viewing point over the harbour provided some consolation. The Garrison Chapel was also demolished to make way for prison officers' homes as was the Military Hospital, which was replaced by an engineering works. The Grand Shaft Barracks were demolished in 1965 and the famous spiral staircase was sealed as a safety measure. In 1967 a new approach road to the prison cut through the North Lines and in 1978 the Prison Department bulldozed a Napoleonic magazine in order to build a boiler house and chimney, which ruined the skyline. This was done without the required consultation with the Department of the Environment and Dover District Council, causing a public outcry and criticism from the Ombudsman following a complaint from the New Dover Group. It happened again in 1990 when the Ombudsman again criticised the Home Office for building a new accommodation block without consultation.

Barrack blocks in the Drop Redoubt (Dover Museum ref d07905)

The Drop Redoubt was opened to the public in 1987 for the first time but only for two weekends staffed by Museum employees and volunteers. The Grand Shaft staircase was restored in 1985 and opened to the public during the summer. An impressive replica entrance was built in Snargate Street in 1995.

Grand Shaft Snargate Street entrance built in 1985 (Dover Museum ref d12101)

Despite the fortifications not occupied by the Home Office being taken over by English Heritage in the early 1990s, little attention has been given to most of this historic site. With English Heritage pleading lack of resources to conserve the complex properly and open it to the public, vandalism and nature are gradually taking over. Volunteer work parties from the Western Heights Preservation Society, formed at the end of the century, try to keep the area tidy.

White Cliffs Countryside Project

Dover District Council owns most of the important ancient chalk grasslands of the Western Heights. They are now cared for by the White Cliffs Countryside Project, which was launched in 1989 with the aim of helping landowners care for the internationally famous cliffs and countryside around Dover and Folkestone. The project is a collaboration between local and county authorities, conservation organisations including English Heritage and the private sector including Eurotunnel. Cattle grazing ceased in the 1950s with the consequent invasion of shrubs and trees threatening the many chalk plant species. Grazing was reintroduced in 1990 and gradually extended whilst the public was still encouraged to walk the slopes, enjoy the landscape, the rare wild flowers and butterflies, using improved footpaths, steps, waymarked routes and guided walks.

Returning to 1959, the retirement of the last of the town's porters, Sidney Tapply, terminated an ancient local office. These porters carried passengers' baggage from the ships to the Customs office and then to an hotel or to transport – and vice versa.

Old Park Mansion was demolished by the Army in 1964. The house was largely rebuilt by Major R B Lawes JP around 1870 but apparently the history of the estate goes back to Edward IV's reign when the Manor of Archer's Court was divided and Little Archer's Court, later called Old Park, was created.

Maud Adamson outside her shop in Strond Street demolished 1966

Construction of the new Townwall Street in the 1960s destroyed a complete medieval arch spanning the Dour, known as the 'Hole in the Wall,' which allowed the river to pass under the town wall on its way to the sea. Another old building disappeared in 1966 when, after a long struggle, DHB obtained permission to demolish the last remaining building in Strond Street, Maud Adamson's little tea shop, believed to be Tudor in origin with a Georgian-style façade. A condition was that the small size bricks should be reused in buildings in Canterbury Cathedral precinct. In the same year the 400 year old offices of Worsfold and Hayward in the Market Square were demolished.

Outside Dover, in 1966, the Ministry of Works decided to preserve and restore the St John Commandery at Swingfield, a 13th century chapel with a 14th century king post roof, which had been part of the adjacent farm buildings. The Ministry of Housing stepped in to prevent the Earl of Guilford from demolishing Waldershare Mansion, built in the early 18th century. It was later converted into flats.

Crabble Corn Mill

In 1971 John Mannering, the owner, offered the derelict Crabble Corn Mill to the Borough Council and/or Kent County Council on condition that the mill was preserved, but as restoration would cost £50,000 it came to nothing, even though in 1958 Kent County Council and Dover Corporation had agreed that Crabble Corn Mill was worthy of preservation. Rebuilt in 1812, it had been 'mothballed' since the end of the 19th century and still had all its machinery intact. Fortunately, the local Cleary Foundation bought it in 1972 for £30,000, repaired it and leased it for a nominal rent to Dover Corporation, which became responsible for its maintenance. It was then opened at times to the public from 1973. In a dangerous state once again in 1983 it was closed and covered in scaffolding to save it from collapse. The cost of restoration was said to be £300,000. Threatened with demolition, the mill was saved in 1987 by the formation of Crabble Corn Mill Trust, which was given the freehold by the

Cleary Foundation plus £25,000 toward restoration. Dover District Council made repairs to the pond wall and gave £130,000 toward refurbishment, which attracted £100,000 from English Heritage. Valiant efforts by the contractors, volunteers, residents of the Young Offenders Institute and Royal Engineers enabled the mill to reopen in 1990 as a working museum. Since then the Trust has struggled to remain solvent amidst controversy about the conduct of its affairs.

The owners of Victoria Park, laid out in the mid 19th century, applied to demolish the fine terrace of houses with stables at the rear, lawns at the front and fine views over the town, but permission was refused and a building preservation order obtained. Dover's

Crabble Corn Mill today

'Tidy Ruin' of old St James' Church, badly damaged during World War II, received a £10,000 facelift. The River Dour Association was formed in 1974 to improve this amenity with Councillor Peter Bean as the first chairman.

Victoria Park overlooking the town centre in 1980

The White Cliffs

The National Trust launched a £250,000 fund to purchase the White Cliffs and save them from development, which it did in 1988. Whilst it meant that car parking charges and fencing were introduced, paths were improved and the chalk downs grassland was preserved by horses grazing. The Saga Visitor Centre on Langdon Cliffs was opened in 1998 by botanist David Bellamy. Three months later the partially turfed roof was blown off the building by 60 miles per hour winds!

There was an outcry in 1978 following the destruction of woodland in the Alkham Valley by Hughie Batchelor who owned Hogbrook Farm. DDC took out tree preservation orders to prevent further clearance but not before the valley was badly scarred. The sudden demolition early one morning in 1988 of Brook House by the owner, the District Council, was considered by many as another act of vandalism. Apparently it would have cost £500,000 to refurbish. It was built as a private residence for William Moxon in about 1860 in what was then Maison Dieu Park which he had acquired. The old Dover Corporation had bought it in 1920 for council offices.

Aerial view of Brook House and its gardens

In 1997 DHB filled in the old stone-lined Patent Slipway at the River Dour end of the Wellington Dock as part of the De Bradelei Wharf development. It was built in 1849 for shipbuilding and repair work and later became part of George Shilson's repair yard.

DDC closed Dover's heritage centre, The White Cliffs Experience off the Market Square, in 2000 because of mounting losses. It had attracted over a million visitors since opening in 1991 at a cost of £14 million. Subsequently plans were announced to hand over the property to KCC for conversion to the Dover Discovery Centre incorporating the adult education centre, the public library, public computer facilities, a café and a theatre.

Characters

RAY WARNER

Ray Warner, photographer extraordinaire, was a gentleman whose work lives on in a series of films about his adopted town of Dover.

Ray was born in Folkestone in November 1914 and educated at the town's Harvey Grammar School. From there, in 1931, he was apprenticed in photography with Lambert Weston where he received the princely sum of 2s 6d (about 13p in 'new' money) a week for the first three years. Always interested in the moving camera, Ray made a film about Folkestone in 1933 whilst still a teenager.

In 1938 he took over, as manager, the Dover-based photographic firm of Dorothy Sherwood in Townwall Street on behalf of Lambert Weston and all seemed set fair for a life among the local business community. The war interrupted normal routine for many people however, including Ray, who joined the Royal Air Force serving with Bomber Command and flying in Lancasters and Halifaxes as a photographer. 'I always remember flying over Cologne after a particularly heavy raid, finding the twin-spired cathedral standing virtually undamaged amid the utmost devastation around it,' said Ray after the war. During this hectic time Ray met Kay, an attractive young WAAF, and they married in Durham.

When the war was over they moved back to Dover with Ray returning to Lambert Weston but going through the turmoil of changing premises with the widening of Townwall Street when his old studio was demolished. A new era began for him when he started trading under his own name.

In 1952 he became a member of Dover Rotary Club and was also, for many years, chairman of the Dover Players initiating Shakespearean productions in the open air at Kearsney Abbey and Dover Castle. He even managed an extra's part in the popular national film about Lady Jane Grey, who reigned for nine days in 1553, parts of which were shot at Dover.

Ray Warner centre with Terry Sutton and Tony Arnold on his right on board 'HMS Albion' off Dover

Ray, when aged 62, retired from his photographic business in 1977 but he continued filming, operating from his home in Castle Avenue. A member of Dover Film Society, he had been collecting clips of Dover since pre-war days and around 1947 started making his own films of the town. In all he produced about

40 annual films depicting the history of the changing face of Dover. He filmed while journalist colleagues wrote the scripts and, in the early days, he also provided the commentary. As his films became more professional and more expensive to produce, he was assisted financially by the Borough Council and later by Dover District Council. The local authority paid for the print while Ray gave his time. As a result, with the district's involvement, his Dover films expanded to take in the whole of the district.

His opportunity to capture up-to-date footage came when he was appointed the BBC's freelance cameraman for the south east area, a very 'newsy' spot in the 50s and 60s with shipwrecks and port expansion. Because he was always such a gentleman Ray was invited to film when other media folk were kept at a distance.

Having already made 25 Dover films, Ray showed his films annually at the Dover Film Festival from 1972 until his untimely death in 1990. His films with Ivan Green's 'Then and Now' presentations attracted thousands to the Town Hall over the years. Fortunately, his cinematic diary of each year remains in the safe custody of Dover Museum where copies of many are still available on video.

1990 Film Festival programme – Ray's last Dover film was shown after his death

Chapter 13

DIGGING UP DOVER'S PAST

The years 1945 to 2000 proved to be a golden age for digging up Dover's past. The town can boast a number of impressive ancient buildings above ground including Dover Castle and the Maison Dieu. Thanks to the work of archaeologists, Dover is now also known for its impressive remains and finds below ground. This was triggered initially by a number of interesting discoveries in the 1950s largely due to preparations for rebuilding on war-damaged sites and followed from 1970 by the largest programme of excavation in any British town.

There has been a settlement in or near Dover since prehistoric times because of its proximity to the continent and the fact that the Dour estuary forms the only significant break in many miles of chalk cliffs providing a haven for shipping. Dover was important to the Romans as a port and since Victorian times it has been known that a harbour wall and possibly baths were buried in the vicinity of the town centre. Bavington Jones' *Perambulation of Dover* published in 1907 mentions a tessellated Roman pavement some ten feet under the market place.

1940s and 50s finds

Towards the end of the Second World War the Dover Excavation Committee was formed with the aim of examining some of the razed sites before rebuilding in an attempt to discover more about the town in the Roman period. As early as 1946 the foundations of chalk built dwellings and a Roman road were unearthed between Queen Street and Market Street. Excavations on other blitzed sites revealed evidence of Roman and medieval buildings. Boys from Dover College and the Boys' Grammar School helped look for and found Roman evidence in the Market Square in 1949. In 1950 portions of a Roman building were uncovered on the west side of Market Square and the remains of other ancient buildings were found under Castle Street. More followed in the rest of the decade including an old well in the centre of the Market Square. A skeleton and bones were found during excavations near the old Market Hall and at Dover College, underneath a 19th century fresco, a much earlier painting of the Last Supper was found, which could have been part of the original decoration of St. Martin's Priory in the 12th century. A new housing site on Long Hill revealed in 1951 a Saxon burial ground containing 170 graves plus coins, swords and ornaments now in the British Museum. Another part of this same burial ground was found in 1994 when 250 graves were discovered. This is one of six Anglo-Saxon burial grounds on the hills above the Dour valley. Part of the Dover Priory cemetery was unearthed at the junction of Folkestone Road and Effingham Street, while workmen digging a trench in Market Street in 1955 unearthed a lead casket containing nearly 700 silver coins. These were valued by the British Museum at £150, which was shared by the two workmen and their foreman.

Excavations for the new National Union of Seamen offices in Snargate Street (Maritime House) revealed portions of two Roman buildings. Both had walls of dressed chalk blocks lined with tufa. The larger had flint foundations overlaid with tiles but covered in a thick layer of soot, whilst the smaller was on a bed of chalk covered by a layer of reddish concrete containing broken tiles. All this is now hidden behind a concrete wall.

The great church and monastery of St Martin le Grand was built originally between 691 and 726, but was destroyed and rebuilt by the Normans. The secular canons were displaced in the twelfth century but the great church served as Dover's mother church until it was destroyed in 1535 as part of Henry VIII's dissolution of the monasteries. Most of the remains disappeared in 1957 with the building of the National Provincial Bank in the Market Square. The mass of flint rubble had been incorporated in a succession of buildings on the site and elsewhere. One find there was a tomb of chalk blocks containing a skeleton thought to be from the 13th century. Perhaps even more interesting were 'pot boiler' flints, used by early man to heat liquids by baking the flints in a fire and then plunging them into the liquid. The tooth of a mammoth perhaps 500,000 years old was yet another find.

In Stembrook large baulks of timber were uncovered about 20 feet below street level, giving the new pub in Stembrook its name, *The Roman Quay*.

1960s

At the Castle the site of an iron age settlement was found under the earthworks in 1962 and Martin Biddle's trench there also revealed a ditch that may have been part of William the Conqueror's early defences.1964 excavations in the cellars of Worsfold and Hayward in the Market Square revealed what was possibly part of the old St Peter's Church..

Kent Archaeological Rescue Unit

Plans for a dual carriageway, now called York Street, in a wide and deep cut in the town centre from the Townwall Street-Snargate Street junction to the bottom of Folkestone Road to remove port traffic from a large section of the shopping area – Bench Street, King Street, Cannon Street and Biggin Street – plus town centre redevelopment was seen by some as a major threat to Roman and other remains. Fortunately, Dover Corporation and the New Dover Group invited the Kent Archaeological Rescue Unit (KARU), led by Brian Philp, to dig on the line of the new road, construction of which involved the destruction of dozens of houses, shops, schools and pubs. An intensive crash programme of excavation and recording, covering some eight acres, was launched in 1970. It also resulted in the level of the new York Street being raised six feet in a last minute battle to avoid damaging the Roman remains below. This was followed by excavating three acres of the ancient town centre ahead of development.

By 1973 KARU staff and its army of volunteers had moved 16,000 tons of soil, concrete and foundations ahead of developers including clearance of a cemetery and demolition of some derelict buildings. The rewards were more than 50 major structures of varying periods, 100,000 significant objects from 4,000 years of domestic rubbish, a fine collection of coins, tiles, brooches, metal fittings, glass and pottery – as well as the most complete Roman fort ever found in southern Britain. Before 1970 none of the archaeological excavation in Dover had really indicated the grand scale and completeness of acres of fine Roman buildings. Many walls still stand, deeply buried, to a height of four to six feet with three major buildings of about nine feet.

By 1973 Brian Philp could say, 'No other Romano-British town can match the completeness of the upstanding civil and military structures such as survive at Dover.' This work went on non-stop until the end of the century with most of the discoveries saved for posterity. It continues, still led by Brian Philp.

Classis Britannica Naval Fort

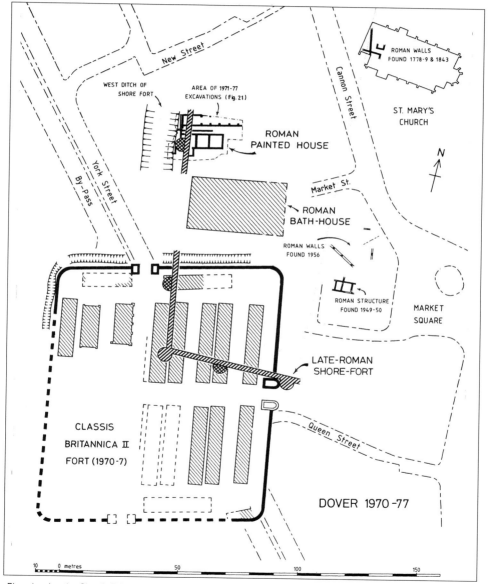

Plan showing the Classic Britannica fort, the site of the Painted House and adjacent Roman buildings (KARU copyright)

The naval fort covered two acres and included 14 major buildings such as a granary and barrack blocks, metalled roads, dozens of drains, sewers and water mains. It was enclosed by a high defensive wall of chalk and tufa fronted by a ditch. Five hundred tile fragments stamped 'CLBR' proved it to be the base of the Romano-British fleet, which used the safe haven of the Dour estuary between the cliffs where Roman lighthouses were built. Evidence of a Roman harbour, comprising substantial timbers, had been found in 1855 under what is now the East Kent bus garage plus the small Roman quay found in the 1950s in Stembrook. Eventually the Roman harbour was blocked by silt and sand dunes. The Roman fleet left Dover soon after 200AD and the naval fort was abandoned.

Roman (Anti-Saxon) Shore Fort

Next a derelict site on the north side of Market Street, designated for a multi-storey car park, which was never built, was excavated, revealing traces not only of a late Roman fort wall, but also the painted wall of a Roman house. Over the next few years the fort wall, the bastion, the defensive ditch to the west and the rooms of the house were revealed. The existence of this fort had been predicted by Sir Mortimer Wheeler in 1929, based on observations by a local man named Amos but it could not be found at that time. In 1970 it was discovered after just two hours only seven feet from Sir Mortimer's predicted line. He celebrated by going out to buy a new hat and from then on was a

Chalk block walls of CLBR fort, cut by the wall of the Anti-Saxon Roman Shore Fort

regular visitor to the excavations. Three hundred feet of the south and west walls were traced, comprising a defensive wall 10 feet thick and 15 feet high, reinforced by great stone bastions at intervals and by a ditch nearly 40 feet wide and ten feet deep.

This fort had been built at the end of the third century AD by the Roman army, centred on Market Street and ignoring the site where the ruins of the second century naval fort stood. It was built to combat the ever increasing Saxon raids.

Anti-Saxon Shore Fort bastion at Queen Street

Roman Painted House

What we now know as The Roman Painted House, off New Street, was one of several found later between the north gate of the Classis Britannica naval fort and the Roman harbour. It proved to be a fine, large house of brick and flint comprising at least six rooms. The large rooms had under-floor heating and the internal walls were plastered and painted in bright colours. Walls in two rooms had survived to six feet high complete with painted plaster. The red mortar floors of the Roman house were only 12 feet below present ground level.

In addition the walls of an earlier, smaller Roman building consisting of at least three rooms was found under what came to be called the Roman Painted House. Beneath the Roman remains were finely worked flint implements of the late Neolithic period, belonging to a settlement which covered the Western Heights' slopes around 2000BC.

The Painted House was erected about 200AD as part of a high quality building, possibly an 'hotel' for notables passing through Dover. With other buildings it formed part of the civil area outside the North Gate of the great Roman naval fort of the Romans' British fleet, the Classis Britannica. In about 270AD the Romans constructed the new (anti-Saxon) shore fort across the area containing the Painted House to replace the old naval fort. The upper section of the house was demolished, a large defensive wall built through two rooms and the rest buried beneath demolition rubble. This catastrophe enabled the paintings to survive. The fort wall and a large bastion are now on display in the Painted House.

Today parts of five important rooms can be seen with thick flint and tile walls, strong concrete floors and under-floor heating. Of special interest are some 400 square feet of finely painted wall plaster, the best-preserved in situ Roman plaster north of the Alps.

Once excavated the Painted House was reburied, but in 1975 it was unearthed and opened for public viewing. 20,000 people visited during the summer. With so much public interest a preservation scheme costing £90,000 was launched. 800 people contributed £5 each which led to Kent County Council and Dover District Council each giving £25,000 and the Department of the Environment

Part of the Roman Painted House

Brian Philp and George Ruck (Chairman of the Painted House Trust) showing the Queen Mother round the Painted House in 1998

£12,500. The Painted House Trust was set up and work began on a building to cover the site. The completed structure cost £74,000 helped considerably by the voluntary effort from the KARU, who undertook site management, supervision of subcontractors, most of the unskilled jobs as well as conservation and graphics. It opened on 12 May 1977 and the scheme soon attracted four national awards.

1986 saw 25,000 fragments of Roman wall reconstructed resulting in wall paintings to ceiling level. The house is open to the public from April to September each year. By 2000 570,000 visitors from all over the world had visited the Painted House including Queen Elizabeth the Queen Mother in 1986.

Other Roman finds

In 1979 one of the biggest and most complete Roman military bathhouses in southern Britain was discovered by the KARU, which was opened to public view temporarily. It was 60 feet by 120 feet with at least 10 rooms and with walls, in a remarkable state of preservation, surviving up to 14 feet high. Part of the south gateway to the Classis Britannica fort was found in Albany Place. In 1983 another large Roman building comprising four rooms with a substantially complete hypocaust system was found and thought to be possibly an extension of the Painted House. Excavations under the derelict Market Hall in the Market Square revealed more Roman remains including a 15 feet high wall presumably built to repel Saxon invaders. An exciting find in 1984 consisted of seven signet ring Roman gemstones, known as intaglios, in a large drain carrying wastewater from the bathhouse. Four more were found the next year, possibly lost by soldiers during their ablutions.

Non-Roman finds

Above the rubble of the Painted House was a large but simple Anglo-Saxon wooden hut built around 800AD. Amongst other finds from later periods were the remains of a Saxon wooden church, 30 feet by 65 feet, possibly the original church of St. Martin dating from the seventh to ninth centuries. The long lost twelfth century nave and south transept of St Martin le Grand church were also found under what was Barwick's yard between Market and Queen Streets. A skeleton encased in lead was found in 1973 off the Market Square, which could have been a Knight of the Crusades. The Zion Chapel site in Queen St revealed a wealthy medieval merchant's house and close by an Elizabethan leather purse containing 11 silver coins.

Controversy

During the 1980s there were plans to extend the Painted House scheme to include the adjacent Roman military bathhouse and the Saxon and Norman churches under a proposed shopping precinct. Planning consent was granted in 1988, but the scheme was overtaken by the plans for the White Cliffs Experience. This created difficulties between the Painted House Trust and KARU on the one hand and the District Council on the other. Despite counter proposals for a more modest Roman Heritage Centre, the grandiose and expensive White Cliffs Experience was built with its foundations penetrating Roman remains. Relations between the various parties were not helped by Dover District Council's decision to bring in archaeologists from Oxford to re-excavate the site for the three floor complex.

Other digs and dives

In 1978 4000 year old flint implements were found in the grounds of Dover College, used by people living there in 2000BC. More remains of St Martin's Priory were also found. In the same year a medieval burial ground was discovered between Priory Road and Biggin Street next to St. Edmund's Chapel. That year divers found the wreck of a ship, believed to be 3000 years old, in Langdon Bay and over the next five years 400 items including axes and other implements, mostly scrap from the continent imported for recasting, were found there. American divers found an almost perfectly preserved wreck of an 18th century British man o' war, HMS Stirling Castle, on the Goodwins in 1980. This 70 gun, three-masted vessel was wrecked in 1703 with the loss of all but 70 of the 440 crew. In 1988 graves found on Priory Hill proved to be part of a large Saxon cemetery.

1994 saw a fine example of continued instant rescue work by KARU. Workmen were digging a new soakaway outside the north door of St. Mary's Church. Joe Harman kept a close eye because he knew that in 1778 Roman walls had been found under the west end of the church. As soon as the ancient remains came to light he alerted staff in the Painted House who arrived within five minutes. Subsequent excavation revealed part of a major Roman building in the churchyard probably comprising at least three rooms with an elaborate underfloor heating system in the main room. A massive mortared wall with many courses composed of Roman tiles, chalk blocks and flints still stood five feet high. Fragments of painted wall plaster are on display in The Painted House.

Canterbury Archaeological Trust

From 1991 two archaeology groups worked in Dover. KARU continued its valuable work (finding, for instance, the home of the Commandant of Classis Britannica at Albany Place comprising two rooms richly decorated with painted walls and the remains of a heating system). Canterbury Archaeology Trust (CAT) team, led by Keith Parfitt, carried out extensive surveys along the route of the proposed Whitfield- Eastry bypass (A256). Evidence of an extensive multi-period complex, mainly Iron Age and Anglo-Saxon, was found at Church Whitfield in 1995 including the remains of a 6th or 7th century Anglo-Saxon hamlet. Other finds along the route included a Bronze Age barrow with at least 11 human burials. In 1998 the CAT maintained a watching brief along the route of a new waste water pipe between Folkestone and the new treatment works at Farthingloe. Amongst the finds was a small Iron Age cremation cemetery at Hougham.

The CAT also worked in advance of the construction of the new A20 from Folkestone to Dover. Three Bronze Age burial mounds were found in Holywell Combe, Folkestone and some evidence of Anglo-Saxon occupation in the 8th and 9th centuries was found at Court Wood near Capel; little was found between Capel and Dover, however. It was a different story at Archcliffe, Limekiln Street and Snargate Street where many remains were found, including post-medieval buildings. Under the York Street roundabout a substantial section of the medieval town wall, surviving to a height of 3.8 metres, 9 metres long and 2.8 metres wide at its base, was found with evidence that the sea once came up to the base of it. The base of an ancient defensive tower and the remains of the medieval town wall were found in Bench Street at its junction with Townwall Street were the remains of Boldware Gate and the adjacent town wall overlain by the foundations of the Three Gun Battery which guarded the river estuary during the 16th and 17th centuries. On the same site were the remains of a massive Roman timber harbour wall. Further to the east the foundations of Butchery Gate tower and a section of wall were also unearthed. At the BP filling station site on Townwall Street in 1996 12th and 13th century chalk-floored timber houses and outbuildings were uncovered with numerous fish bones and hooks suggesting that it was a fishermen's settlement. These and other excavations greatly informed the post-Roman history of Dover and completed the story of how the haven was created and used. Further inland, excavations in the Ladywell car park revealed the remains of medieval buildings, which were part of the Maison Dieu.

Bronze Age Boat

The exciting discovery of the Bronze Age Boat in September 1992 was the culmination of a year's work by CAT on the line of the new A20. It was a unique and unprecedented find that captured the imagination of people not only in Dover and Britain, but around the world. Buried six metres below the streets of Dover was an oak boat about 3,600 years old, perfectly preserved by a bed of peat washed by fresh water, found during the construction of the pedestrian underpass beneath the A20 at the end of Bench Street. It is thought that about two-thirds of the vessel was eventually revealed (9 metres long by 2.3 metres wide), after more excavations were authorised with a total probable length of 14 metres. The craft had to be lifted, otherwise the underpass construction would destroy it. The CAT team working with the contractors and staff from Dover Museum, Dover Harbour Board and English Heritage cut the craft into sections and lifted it, watched by crowds of people. It was then stored safely in a water tank to inhibit decay where 3,000 people viewed it during one weekend. A six-year

The site of the Bronze Age Boat excavation in Townwall Street

study programme involving 30 specialists followed, including a reconstruction of a mid-section, using facsimiles of Bronze Age tools. The capabilities of the boat, the water it could travel in, the cargoes and crew numbers were all studied. The workmanship was superb. There is a strong suggestion that it was a sea-going craft (possibly the first cross Channel ferry) and, if so, the earliest example in the world.

In addition to the study programme a scheme for the preservation of the timbers and eventual display to the public had to be considered. In October 1993 the Dover Bronze Age Boat Trust was formed with the aim of preserving and

Excavating the Bronze Age Boat

displaying the boat in Dover. All the trustees were local – from Dover's leading businesses and organisations, Dover District Council and the Canterbury Archaeological Trust. The boat was donated to the Trust by the Department of Transport. A bid for £1.2 million from the Heritage Lottery Fund was successful and with other grants and donations the preservation work began. The sections were soaked for a year in a water soluble wax to impregnate the ancient wood, which would be hardened later by freeze drying. A team from the Mary Rose Trust arrived in Dover in August 1995 and, assisted by the CAT, packed the timbers for their journey to the Mary Rose laboratories at Portsmouth. Three years later the timbers returned to Dover. In the meantime the planning and building of the display gallery took place. Whilst Dover District Council was unable to contribute substantial funds to the project, it allowed Museum staff to treat it as a priority, provided the space for the gallery plus a 25 years commitment to finance the boat's display and its essential air conditioning. When the timbers returned three years later, in August 1998, the 32 pieces were reassembled painstakingly on to a special cradle, watched by the public through viewing panels. The display of the boat involved model makers, graphic designers, software designers, pre-historic hut builders and others in order to explain not only the story of the boat but also the Bronze Age period. By the autumn of 1999 the reassembly and the fitting out of the gallery in the Museum was completed and on 22 November 1999 the Lord Lieutenant of Kent opened it, watched by many of the 150 people who had worked on the project. Today the Bronze Age Boat Gallery is an established feature of Dover's heritage attractions.

Chapter 14

LORD WARDENS OF THE CINQUE PORTS

Edward the Confessor introduced Ship Service requiring the five ('cinque' pronounced 'sink') ports of Dover, Sandwich, Hythe, New Romney and Hastings to provide ships and men to the Crown in return for certain rights and privileges, which made the ports self governing with their own courts and taxes as well as being exempt from the King's taxes. Later, the two 'antient towns' of Winchelsea and Rye were added. Representatives or 'Barons' also had the right to carry a canopy over the monarch at coronations and to sit at his or her right side at coronation feasts. William the Conqueror confirmed these arrangements. Dover's contribution originally was to provide 20 ships each with 21 men for 15 days a year free of charge with another 15 days provided, if necessary, at the expense of the monarch. The Confederation of the Cinque Ports was at the zenith of its powers at the beginning of the 14th century, but began to decline with the birth of a proper Royal Navy. Today, of the original seven only Dover remains a major port.

The post of Lord Warden of the Cinque Ports dates from the early 13th century. Originally the prime function was to act as admiral of the Cinque Ports' fleet in time of war, but it also provided direct communication for the king with these ports and also gave the portsmen a leader enabling them to act together and to influence the king. From the 11th century the two primary defences for SE England were Dover Castle and the Cinque Ports' ships, originally under separate command. Hubert de Burgh, Constable (governor) of Dover Castle successfully defended the Castle against the French in 1216 and in the following year took charge of the Cinque Ports' fleet and defeated the French fleet. From then on the Constables were also appointed Lord Warden with the task of ensuring that the King's commands were carried out by the portsmen, but also undertaking to defend the charter rights and liberties of the Cinque Ports. By the end of the 14th century the post became an appointment for life. Today the post is now largely ceremonial.

There were three Lord Wardens of the Cinque Ports and Constables of Dover Castle in the last half of the twentieth century. Sir Winston Churchill was offered the appointment during the 1939-45 war but he was far too busy to visit Dover for his installation until 1946.

When he died, aged 90, he was succeeded in 1965 by Sir Robert Menzies (later Lord Menzies) who, as Prime Minister of Australia, had proved such a great ally during the war. Ivan Green recalls that after Sir Robert's installation he asked Ivan to accompany him for several days in his chauffeur-driven car on a tour of the Cinque Ports and to tell him something about the historic towns. Ivan found it most enjoyable except that, 'I could not keep up with Sir Robert's drinking!' During his wardenship Sir Robert visited Dover several times, especially when it gave him the opportunity to watch cricket at Canterbury and elsewhere. In 1968 he received a warm welcome when he took the salute at a military tattoo at Crabble Athletic Ground.

Sir Winston Churchill at Dover Castle ready for his installation as Lord Warden in 1946

James A. Johnson with Sir Robert Menzies at Dover Castle for his installation as Lord Warden in 1965

Following Sir Robert's death everyone was delighted when the Queen appointed her mother, Elizabeth the Queen Mother, to the joint posts, the first woman in history to be made Lord Warden. She was installed in Dover on 1 August 1979 when her smile beat the black clouds and rain. Dover had not seen such pageantry for many years. The town, port and garrison joined with State and Church to welcome the new Lord Warden, who arrived on the Royal Yacht *Britannia*. Thousands crowded the decorated streets to watch the Household Cavalry

The Queen Mother at her installation as Lord Warden in 1979

The Queen Mother during one of her regular visits to Dover

escort the carriage procession from Dover Castle, to the Grand Court of Shepway, convened in a large marquee in the grounds of Dover College. At her installation the Queen Mother vowed to protect the franchises, liberties and customs of the Cinque Ports whilst guns boomed out from Dover Castle and the RAF flew overhead. After the ancient and colourful ceremony the Queen Mother walked in sunshine through the huge crowds to the Town Hall followed by 200 delegates of the Confederation of the Cinque Ports and other guests. Typically, she stopped to chat to patients from the hospital.

She made regular visits to the Dover area, usually weekending at her official residence at Walmer Castle a few days before her birthday. She attended the official opening in May 1993 of the Battle of Britain memorial at Capel and was in Dover in July 2000, a few days before her 100th birthday, when a giant birthday card was presented to her. During her visits she often attended matins at the church of St Mary in Castro and occasionally at St Mary the Virgin in Dover of which, as Lord Warden, she was one of three patrons.

Characters

IVAN GREEN

Ivan Green is well known in Dover, Kent and beyond as a respected historian, author of many local history books and a lecturer. His *Then and Now* presentations were an integral part of the Dover Film Festival throughout its life.

He had to study the hard way, working his way through college away from home to gain an engineering degree. He met Margaret and she married him, homeless and penniless, in 1935 and so began a lifelong partnership and mutual interest in history. Ivan's first job was as an assistant lecturer but when war came in 1939 they both volunteered.

Margaret spent the war as an ambulance driver in London. Most of Ivan's war service was spent in the desert servicing armoured vehicles but when he suffered major injuries and was no longer fit for such duties he became a political officer in the Jordan desert living as an Arab for two years.

After the war, Ivan's working life was spent in education, retiring as Deputy Head of Archer's Court School in Dover in 1977. Many former pupils remember building go-karts with him. During his career he served for 8 years on a committee of the government's School Council and was elected national president of his professional organisation. He was a member of several professional bodies and was an associate member of the Institute of British

Ivan Green celebrating the launch of his latest book 'Dover and the Monarchy' in 2001 with Merril Lilley, Derek Leach and Ken Wraight

Engineers. For his Open University BA he read medieval history, the history of art and architecture and the English industrial revolution.

It was also after the war that Ivan and Margaret began collecting photographs and data, which now includes some 45,000 colour slides, over 50,000 black and white negatives and many volumes of information. They have recorded on film and typescript every town and village, every castle and parish church, most of the great public and private buildings, rivers and natural phenomena of Kent, their much-loved adopted county. This large collection has provided the material for ten of their twenty books recording aspects of Dover and Kent. The *Book of the Cinque Ports* has become a standard work. Ivan's twenty-third book, *Dover and the Monarchy from Conquest to Revolution 1066 to 1688* was published by The Dover Society in 2001. Over the years he also gave more than 800 lectures and published some 700 articles.

Now in the evening of his days and without his beloved wife, Ivan is not in good health and is mainly confined to his home but continues to write – working on his next book about 19th century Dover.

Chapter 15

THE GARRISON

For more than a thousand years Dover has been a garrison town because of its strategic position. However, modern weapon technology and the so-called 'peace dividend' with the ending of the Cold War helped strip Dover of much of its military presence. In 1950 the town still had three regimental battalions based in its barracks. At times, in the next 50 years, there were up to 3,000 troops stationed there, but by the turn of the century the garrison was reduced to one battalion of around 600 men and women.

The ending of the Cold War, with a possible conflict with Communist Russia, meant fewer troops were needed in the Army and Dover suffered from the ensuing amalgamations of regiments. Rocket science resulted in a drastic reduction in the strength of coastal defence batteries and many of the guns that once defended Dover and the soldiers who manned them were removed.

During the last 50 years Dover lost three of its four barracks. Dover Castle became a tourist attraction, blocks at the Western Heights were demolished and Old Park Barracks, built in 1939, came into the possession of DHB and was redesignated Port Zone. By the turn of the century only Connaught Barracks remained.

The town was often left with virtually no troops as battalions went off to deal with a series of crises including the Berlin blockade, Malaya, the Suez Canal,

A sea front parade in about 1950 with Bill Fish, Mayor, on the saluting base

Cyprus, the Falklands and the Gulf. In 1953, for instance, it was the third time since the Second World War that Dover had no troops when trouble brewed with the Mau Mau in Kenya.

Long range guns defending the town were being broken up in 1957, the coastal artillery disbanded and the railway network serving the gun sites dismantled. In the same year the Home Guard, re-formed because of the threat from Russia, was again disbanded.

A sign of the diminishing size of the Dover garrison was the demolition in 1962 of the Garrison Church, a landmark at the Western Heights for more than 100 years. Two years later, in 1964, Old Park Mansion was demolished to make

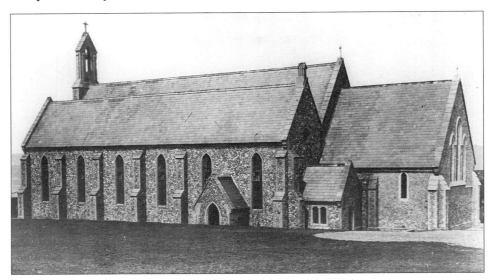

Garrison Church Western Heights demolished 1962

way for a new army church at the barracks there. Old Park Barracks and Connaught Barracks were reconstructed. In 1967 the old officers' mess, with its green landmark dome, at Connaught Barracks was badly damaged by fire and the following year was demolished and a new mess constructed on the same site.

In the late 1960s Dover people enjoyed a series of military tattoos at various venues including Crabble Athletic Ground.

It came as a shock in 1973 when it was revealed that the future of Old Park Barracks, by now the home of the Junior Leaders Regiment, Royal Engineers, was in doubt. Plans were in hand to transfer the regiment to Chepstow, but that idea was shelved for financial reasons in 1976.

In 1974 the army announced plans to build 288 married family homes at Guston named Burgoyne Heights. The Queen visited the Royal Green Jackets at Connaught Barracks in 1975. The strength of the Junior Leaders at Old Park reached 700 and in 1977 Lt. Colonel John Blashford-Snell, later to be a renowned explorer, was the Commanding Officer.

A new Territorial Army headquarters was built, and opened in 1980, on the site of the Odeon cinema in London Road. It had moved from the sea front to make way for dock road widening. In the same year work started on a £1 million rebuild of Connaught Barracks.

As feared, in 1984 came confirmation that the Junior Leaders Regiment at Old Park was to be amalgamated with the Apprentices College at Chepstow later in the decade. At that time the young soldiers' regiment topped 600, with 140 permanent staff and 100 civilian employees. The regiment had been stationed at Old Park for 32 years; the last Commanding Officer was Lt. Colonel Graham Chilton RE. The end came in 1991 when the War Office said Old Park was 'not a suitable place for a replacement unit.'

Controversy followed when it was revealed in 1986 that the army was planning to buy 308 acres in the Alkham Valley for military training to replace land lost for the Channel Tunnel, but such was the outcry that the idea was dropped.

Constable's Tower at Dover Castle, throughout all the changes, has remained the home of the Deputy Constable who is also the local army commander.

Constable's Tower

Deputy Constable

The post of Deputy Constable of Dover Castle – deputy to the Lord Warden of the Cinque Ports, who is also Constable of the Castle – has been held over the years by high-ranking officers whose normal term of office these days is about three years. Centuries ago the appointment of Constable, when castles were vital for controlling the area, was more important than that of Lord Warden.

During the 55 years covered by this book, the office of Deputy Constable has been held by a series of important military men who, to varying degrees, have played a major rôle in the life of the town. At the war's end, in 1945, Brigadier H C Pickering was in post, succeeded swiftly in the following year by Colonel A T Somerset and Major-General H C Stockwell and then by Major-Generals P G Gregson-Ellis and Bernard Kimmins in 1950, E O Herbert in 1952 and R King in 1953. In 1956 Major-General King, then Commander of the Home Counties District, was appointed Director of Quartering and was succeeded by Major-

General W F Turner for three years. He departed in 1959 when Major-General Paul Gleadell was appointed. When he left his Constable's Tower residence in 1961, Major-General Tony Grimshaw, who had commanded the Royal Inniskilling Fusiliers at Dover in 1953, succeeded him. Major-General Francis Wyldbore-Smith proved a popular Deputy Constable when he was appointed in the summer of 1965.

Then the rank of the Deputy Constable was changed from Major-General to Brigadier as the British army slimmed down in numbers. Fewer soldiers meant fewer in the senior ranks! Brigadier John Watson Badcock was appointed in January 1968 and, during that year, entertained Sir Robert Menzies, who was by then Lord Warden of the Cinque Ports. Brigadier Tony Findlay succeeded Brigadier Badcock in 1970 and, three years later, he was followed by Brigadier Neil Fletcher. Another popular appointment was that of Brigadier Maurice Atherton, who became the 200th Deputy Constable in 1976. Brigadier Atherton, now living at Barham in retirement, still takes a great interest in Dover and is President of The Dover Society. He was followed by Brigadiers R T P Hume, Michael Lee in 1984, Richard Webster in 1987, John Holman in 1989, Guy de Vere Wentworth Hayes in 1992 and David Godsal in 1995, who served until Trevor Minter was appointed in 1998. He was in post during the Millennium year, but Brigadier David Santa Olalla took up residence in the ancient Constable's Tower in 2001as the 208th Deputy Constable of Dover Castle.

Chapter 16

CHURCHES

Between 1945 and 2000 parishes amalgamated, churches were repaired or demolished and there was a reduction in the number of clergy as well as some extensions and new churches. A positive development was the increasing co-operation between all the denominations, coordinated by the efforts of the Dover Christian Council, later renamed Christians Together in Dover.

In 1945 most of Dover's church buildings were showing signs of war damage. Its only synagogue, in Northampton Street, was so badly wrecked it was demolished and those of the Jewish faith had to worship in other towns. In 1947 the Salvation Army moved back into a temporary Citadel building in the High Street while London Road Methodist Church re-opened after damage suffered in September 1944 by enemy shells. The Pier District church of Holy Trinity,

Holy Trinity Church

consecrated in 1835, was demolished in 1949 whilst Wesley Methodist Church in Folkestone Road was re-built and came into use again. Old St James' Church, built before 1291, in St James' Street next to the *White Horse* public house, was very badly damaged during the war and in 1950 a large section collapsed. Demolition workers had to be called in to make the rest of the building safe. Today what is left is retained as a tidy ruin. Two years later Charlton Church was re-hallowed after war damage and the Unitarian Church in Adrian Street was re-opened for services.

As much of Dover's pre-war crowded downtown population moved to new housing estates on the outskirts, or in the villages, several churches were declared redundant. Despite strong opposition new St James' Church in Maison Dieu

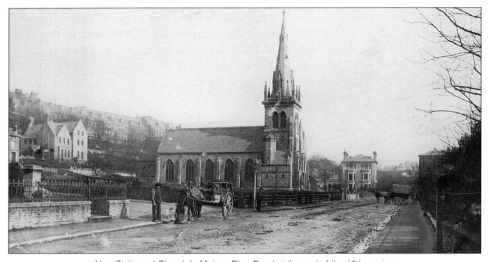

New St James' Church in Maison Dieu Road at the end of the 19th century

Road was demolished in 1952-1953.This attractive building, with a 144 foot high spire and cross, was constructed for £10,000 to accommodate up to 1,400 worshippers and consecrated in 1862. Further inland the war-wrecked church of 50 year old St Barnabas in Barton Road was pulled down while the civil authorities gave consent to the rebuilding of the badly damaged Salvation Army Citadel, which was completed in 1955.

In 1955 the foundation stone of the new River Methodist Church was laid and the church, in Lewisham Road, was opened in 1956. In 1958 a new meeting house for the Quakers was opened in Maison Dieu Road. A new Roman Catholic church on the Buckland Estate, Our Lady of Dover, was dedicated in 1960 as was a new Anglican church, St Nicholas, in the same area. Snargate Street Methodist chapel, next to the Grand Shaft, and dating from 1834 was closed in 1960.

In 1967 the Jehovah Witnesses built their own church, with their own hands, on Military Road. The same year an appeal was launched by Catholic priest, Father Terence Tanner, to restore the 13th century St Edmund's Chapel in Priory Road. The appeal was successful and the restored chapel was re-consecrated in 1968 with occasional services still held there.

The reconsecration of St Edmund's Chapel in 1968

St Bartholomew's Church

Christ Church

Elders at Salem Baptist church in Biggin Street, next to *The Queen's Head* public house, decided to sell their 125 year old chapel to Boots the Chemist and moved to a purpose built church in Maison Dieu Road in 1970. In 1971 Dover members of the Congregational and Presbyterian denominations met and decided, as elsewhere in the country, to amalgamate and become the United Reformed Church, worshipping at the High Street church.

In 1974 another landmark Dover church was demolished. The Church Commissioners had decided early in the year that St Bartholomew's Church in Templar Street, just off London Road, was redundant and demolition started a few months later. The building, constructed in 1874 at a cost of £7,500, had seating for 750 worshippers. The site was used to build flats. During the same year £15,000 was spent at St Mary's Church, removing the mayor's and the Trinity House pilots' galleries and improving the entrance at the tower end.

The Church Commissioners in 1977 decided that the 133 year old Christ Church in Folkestone Road, where services had ceased in 1973, was no longer needed. The building was demolished, the site sold for flats and the parish merged with neighbouring St Martin's. Wesley Methodist Church in Folkestone Road was declared redundant in 1981 and was bought by Dover College for use as a hall.

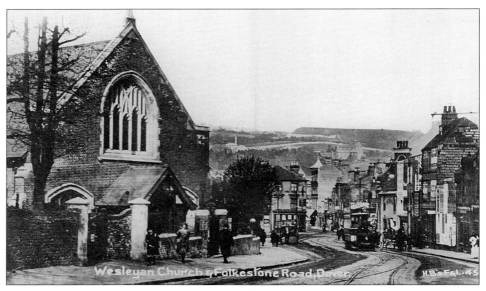

Wesley Methodist Church, Folkestone Road early in the 20th century

The Ark, Noah's Ark Road

One denomination showing signs of growth was the Apostolic Church. In 1960 planning approval was given for a new church for them at the corner of Erith Street and Buckland Terrace and construction began the same year. Soon their church was not big enough and they moved some services to premises in the town centre until a completely new church, The Ark, was built at Noah's Ark Road in 1996 on the site of the former isolation hospital.

Tubby Clayton, the 81 year old founder of TocH, visited Dover in 1968 to open TocH's new Dover HQ in the crypt of the Unitarian Church. The ecumenical TocH did useful work during this period. Founded in 1915 by Rev Tubby Clayton, who created a home from home for allied soldiers in Belgium, it has branches worldwide but mainly in Britain. Membership is open to anyone prepared to 'build bravely, love widely, think fairly and to witness humbly.' This translates into projects to rehabilitate prisoners and to improve the conditions of life for the young, the poor and the sick such as hospital broadcasting, SOS alarms for the elderly, summer projects for children, holidays for children in need, work with the handicapped and elderly. The Buckland Branch was formed in 1937 although there had previously been a Maxton branch. It met first in the premises of Jenkins and Pain at the bottom of Union Road (now Coombe Valley Road), then in St Edmund's Chapel and finally at the Unitarian Church before its demise toward the end of the century. Local activities included Borstal boys chopping wood for pensioners, the flashing light alarm system for the housebound and regular visits to the residents of both Chartham and Eastry hospitals.

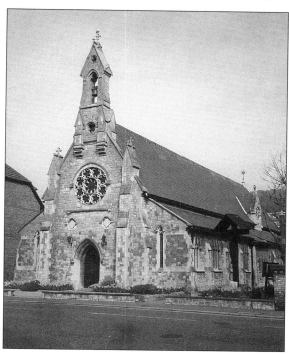

St Paul's Roman Catholic Church

In 1965, for the first time, Roman Catholics joined other Dover denominations for a united service at the Town Hall. In 1987 an arsonist, who was later convicted, caused a disastrous fire at St Paul's RC Church (built in 1867-68) in Maison Dieu Road. Catholic worshippers were welcomed into the Anglican church of St Mary the Virgin to hold their services according to their own traditions. The result was a closer friendship between the two denominations. In the same year women in the Church of England began taking Holy Orders and one of the first in Kent was Miss Marjorie Cobb, a deaconess attached to St Mary's, Dover.

The 'Soup Kitchen' was started in 1990 when Stephanie Perrow of River Methodist Church decided to do something to meet the needs of the homeless living rough in Dover by providing food and drink for them every evening. With a handful of other church members she set out to feed them but initially failed to find them since they were all bedded down and out of sight in the evening. Steph persisted and soon Social Services were referring people to the 'soup kitchen,' which opened at 6pm and operated from the boot of a car. Other churches were contacted and each agreed to cover one day of the week throughout the year. Later a portakabin was obtained to use as a base in Russell Street car park. Now the project involves about 200 helpers, including some non churchgoers, on a rota basis. Customer numbers vary from six to 26 each evening and food includes tea, coffee (both with lots of sugar), soup, sandwiches, pies, pasties and toasted sandwiches. Essential items such as sleeping bags, anoraks and gloves are donated and appreciated. This valuable service still goes on every evening. The homeless are not forgotten at Christmas with Steph and a small band of helpers providing Christmas and Boxing Day dinners at a town centre church. All this is provided free of charge by those involved with the help of voluntary donations.

Christians from churches in Dover and Folkestone took part in a special edition of the BBC television programme Songs of Praise broadcast live from both ends of the Channel Tunnel in 1994. In 1995 150 people attended an ecumenical service to mark the 700th anniversary of the martyrdom of Thomas de la Hale killed in Dover Priory. Plans to extend River Parish Church to accommodate the growing congregation caused controversy not only within the congregation but also among the residents of River. The plans were finally approved   in 1997 by an ecclesiastical court and an attractive extension in keeping with the original building was constructed. The bells of St Mary's rang out in 1998 to mark the launch of a £100,000 bells' restoration appeal.

London Road Methodist Church

By the end of the century there was uncertainty about the future of some of the town centre churches. London Road Methodists were considering replacing their large 100 year old church with something more suitable for today and the Anglicans were having to face a reduction in the number of clergy.

Dover Christian Council/Christians Together in Dover

Christians from various denominations working together made a substantial contribution to church activity over the last 30 years of the century. Dover Christian Council was formed in 1971 with Rev Berkeley Johnson, minister of

Salem Baptist Church, as its first chairman, but it was not affiliated to any national organisation. The Council had a mixed reception amongst the local churches ranging from cooperation to apathy and opposition. Amongst its early achievements and still popular today was the annual carol concert, Come Christmas Carolling, at the Town Hall, which it took over from the Salvation Army when it was unable to continue organising it. Another annual event, which has stood the test of time, is the Week of Prayer for Christian Unity with its agape meal. The Dover Christian Chronicle is also still distributed to Christians throughout the Dover area. The Vicar of St Martin's and Sister Anne of St Ursula's organised a holiday in Dover for children from troubled Northern Ireland. Half the children were Protestant and half Roman Catholic. The Council was revived in the early 80s and has gone from strength to strength ever since. The annual series of Michael Mummery Lectures began then as well as the Good Friday Walk of Witness when Christians process through the town centre following the Cross, with several stops for readings, prayers and hymns, before climbing the 64 Steps to erect three crosses on the Western Heights overlooking the town. The 10 mile sponsored walk for Christian Aid also became a popular annual event. In 1994 the name was changed to Christians Together in Dover, reflecting the growing desire of the different churches to do more things together including an open air sunrise service on the Western Heights on Easter Sunday.

From 1999 a number of local organisations helped asylum seekers in the town with Christians providing facilities including English lessons and a drop-in centre. Dover churches joined the Jubilee 2000 campaign to abolish Third World debt to celebrate the Millennium.

1993 Good Friday Walk of Witness at journey's end, Western Heights

A most notable achievement at the end of the century was the ecumenical open air service in Dover College grounds followed by the peace light lantern procession to the sea front by some three thousand people on New Year's Eve 1999 celebrating 2,000 years since Christ's birth and signalling two days of Millennium celebrations.

Characters

JACK HEWITT

Now an active 90 year old, Jack Hewitt has given a lifetime of service to his fellow men, mainly, but not only, through his very many years in the scout movement and in the Order of St John. In both organisations he held and holds high office locally and was held in high esteem nationally. His 29 years in the County Ambulance Service also enabled Jack to serve through his paid work, which he loved and for which he was commended several times. He was awarded the MBE in 1996.

Fund raising ideas come naturally to Jack. 'Perhaps the simplest was when I sat on a bench with a clipboard and just kept quiet. Passers-by asked what I was doing and I told them what I was raising money for and I raised over £100!'

Jack Hewitt, awarded the MBE in the 1996 New Year Honours

Jack has also travelled widely all over the world, both as a courier for many years for Raymond Cook Tours and as a seeker of unusual experiences in far flung parts of the world. To celebrate the Millennium Jack, aged 88, joined an expedition to Antarctica! Many of these holidays have enabled him to see members of St John in action in other countries. Seeking new experiences has been a lifelong aim, whether flying across the Channel as a young man or taking a hot air balloon ride on his 80th birthday!

His life story, *Greetings, Dover!* included many amusing and hair raising anecdotes, some of which are hard to believe, but Jack insists that they are true. The son of a Dover baker, Jack would visit the local grocer and on one occasion when he was ten he asked for broken biscuits but was told there weren't any. So

Jack kicked a box of biscuits over and said, 'You have now!' He is a cheeky chappy and has often 'got away with murder,' particularly during his war service, in order to have his way or to do what he thought was right. This cheeky chappy is also a cheerful chappy. He is often about town even now giving a cheerful word to everyone he meets, always beginning, of course, with 'Greetings!' Needless to say, anybody who has met Jack cannot forget that laugh of his.

Chapter 17

CLUBS AND SOCIETIES

Most, if not all, of Dover's clubs and societies suspended activities during World War II. Some resumed after; others did not, but new organisations were formed giving Dover a rich variety of societies catering for different hobbies and interests all of which contribute to the feeling of community in the town. This and the following three chapters mention some, but by no means all of them.

In 1946 the new Conservative Club opened in Castle Hill House replacing the Carlton Club destroyed in 1942. The Dover Film Society was reformed in 1947 by some teachers from Dover College. The YMCA opened a residential club at Godwynehurst in 1949 and the Royal Society of St George was revived. Cobham House Girls' Club closed after eight years in 1950 and Charlton Green Youth Club became mixed. A Sea Rangers Company, led by Lillian Kay, met at the Seamen's Club and sailed round the harbour in a converted ship's lifeboat, *SRS Stella Polaris*. A new Working Men's Club on the corner of Erith Street replaced their Snargate Street premises.

The Dover branch of the Red Cross was reformed in 1951 and in 1952 the Boy Scouts' Association opened its Dover HQ in Curzon Road after over 25 years of fund raising. An unusual group formed in 1952 and still going strong is the Dover & Deal branch of the Maidstone and District and East Kent Bus Club, membership of which is open to anybody with an interest in buses. The new HQ of St John Ambulance opened on Military Road in 1954, replacing the old war-damaged HQ in the former Christ Church School.

In 1955 *TS Lynx*, the HQ of the Dover Sea Cadets, was dedicated although it had been open for some years. The Dover branch of the Association of Men of Kent and Kentish Men was revived. The Dover Philatelic Society was formed as was the Lifeboat Ladies Guild, which raises so much money for the Lifeboat Service.

The Church of England Soldiers' Sailors' and Airmen's Institute bought the Cedars Hotel in Maison Dieu Road in 1956 to convert into a seamen's club and a Ship Spotters' Club started with two lookout points at Archcliffe and Admiralty Pier.

1957 was a big year for Scouts celebrating 50 years of the movement and the birth of their founder, Baden-Powell. A service was held in the Odeon Cinema and a Golden Jubilee Fête in Connaught Park. The St John Ambulance Association also celebrated 50 years in Dover.

1958 was quite a year for the start of new clubs: the East Kent Rambling Club, a roller skating club using the Liverpool Street drill hall and later the sea cadets' hall, Dover Beekeeping Society and a local Natural History Society. The Rotary Club organised a Citizen at Leisure exhibition in the Town Hall, showing how Dover people spent their leisure time. It attracted 5,000 visitors over the three days. Dover WVS celebrated its 21st anniversary in 1959. In the following year the Dover youth club had to leave its Charlton Green premises to make way for extensions to Dover Engineering Works; fortunately, alternative premises were found in Barton Road.

1960 was yet another good year for new clubs: Dog Handling and Training Club, Record and Dance Club, Tape Recording Club, Cine Club, Dover branch of the Campaign for Nuclear Disarmament and an ex (Round) Tablers' Club. More unusual was the Go-Kart Club formed after demonstrations of go-karts made locally. The track was on land at St Radigund's. The YMCA launched an appeal in 1961 for £10,000 to build and equip a youth club at Godwynehurst.

The Oddfellows

Oddfellows Club and Institute with Murdoch's

The oldest club in Dover, the Oddfellows Club and Institute, refurbished its Pencester Road premises in 1961. The name goes back to the 14th century when people from a variety of trades banded together for common support. Called officially, The Loyal Cinque Ports Warden Lodge, a Dover lodge met first at the *Fox Inn* in St James' Street in 1800 'to raise a common stock of money in readiness for the relief of the several members in all cases of sickness and death' and met in various places such as the Wellington Hall in Snargate Street and the *Walmer Castle* in Market Square before purchasing its Pencester Road premises in 1866. They were badly damaged during World War II, but the sick visitors still visited ill members every week during the war. After the introduction of the National Health Service in 1948 it became difficult to retain and to recruit new members. Ladies were accepted in 1951 and membership stood at 1400 in 1952.Today, this mutual non-profit friendly society still helps members in need with help for optical and dental costs and other benefits as well as organising social events for members to enjoy.

New Dover Group

The New Dover Group held its first meeting in 1964. It was the brainchild of David Ennals the local MP and was formed to act as a watchdog over redevelopment. It took an active interest in planning, transport, education, history and archaeology, playing an important part in starting the Dover digs off Market Square to save Roman remains from the York Street development. It helped organise the 1965 Town Hall history exhibition, the Riverside walk campaign and Dover by-pass campaign. Following a town survey it produced a plan and model of Dover in the year 2000! Doug Crellin, Collector of Customs & Excise and well-known in the town, was a chairman as was Jack Woolford. At its height there were several hundred members, but without any social programme interest waned and the New Dover Group went into 'suspended animation' in 1981.

Motorbikes were very popular and large groups of bikers used to gather in various parts of the town. Father Bill Shergold founded the 69 Club for them, having previously founded the 59 Club in London. Charlton Church was quite a sight when they attended his services. The club still meets at the *Old Endeavour* in London Road.

The fund raising for charity club, Dover Lions, was formed in 1971 and has provided the town with fun events ever since, including an annual firework display in Connaught Park.

Dover History Society

The present Dover History Society was formed in 1971 and Ivan Green, a founder member, remembered its early days. Miss Kathleen George, who attended Ivan's history lectures, had the original idea and spoke to Mrs Sylvia Corrall, the Reference Section Librarian. A meeting, chaired by the Mayor, George Lock, was called to discuss the idea, attended by Sylvia Corrall, Kathleen George, Lillian Kay, Ivan Green, Terry Sutton and one or two others. There was a discussion about what to call the new society – Dover Historical or Dover History Society. Ivan's view prevailed that it could only be Dover History – it was not yet historical! Everybody put 10/- in the kitty to launch the new enterprise. Mrs Corrall was the first Chairman and, when she moved away, Joe Harman took over and remains chairman.

The monthly lectures were first held in Charlton Church Hall. The Society never looked back with up to 150 attending lectures until the formation of the Dover Society and Friends of the Museum affected numbers. 1984 was a highlight when the History Society hosted the annual conference of the Kent Federation of History Societies and organised a series of lectures in the morning followed by guided tours in the afternoon.

There were two outings each year. Initially an old coach was used, run by a member who was also the Unitarian Church pastor, but later Ayers Coaches were hired, whose drivers used to vie with each other to drive the coach on these outings. Ivan was the organiser and guide for these Kent tours for several years. He and Margaret always prepared two versions for each tour – wet and dry! On one occasion a lady said that Ivan must know every public toilet in Kent and he replied, 'Madam, in my position I have to!'

Dover Transport Museum

It was in 1980 that a small group of transport enthusiasts formed a society, which became the Dover Transport Museum in 1983. George Pitts was the first chairman. The Museum's first home was Dover Waterworks on Connaught Road, but when the water company was sold the Transport Museum was forced to move, finding a home in one of Dover Harbour Board's workshops in Cambridge Road. With the premises required for the De Bradelei factory shops development, the Museum moved yet again in 1994 to Old Park Barracks, which had been

Members of Dover Transport Museum clebrate its move to Old Park in 1994

bought by Dover Harbour Board. At the end of the century the Museum was fighting to raise sufficient money to buy the freehold of its premises to avoid eviction. It owns many of its vehicles, restoring them as necessary, whilst some are owned by members. The vehicles may be seen not only at the Transport Museum but also at fêtes and other events in the area. The Waldershare Vintage Weekend, organised by the Museum, was popular for several years.

The local youth groups combined in an ambitious venture in 1982 when they bought shares in a Dover-based Kent Venture Boat Trust project. A Dutch barge was bought for £4,500 and refitted as an adventure holiday home for youngsters. In the same year the Dover Community Association's move from Pencester Road to 1, Maison Dieu Road caused a row when local residents objected but to no avail.

The Dover Society

Following an initiative by Philomena Kennedy, The Dover Society was formed in 1988 with a number of objectives: to promote high standards of planning and architecture; to inform the public about the geography, history, archaeology and

Cowgate Cemetery following restoration

architecture of Dover; to secure the preservation and improvement of features of historic or public interest; and a belief that a good environment is a good investment. These objectives are pursued by a programme of monthly meetings with speakers, outings, restoration projects such as the regular work parties in Cowgate Cemetery, three newsletters a year for its 400 members, publishing or supporting the publication of books of local interest, monitoring all planning proposals and putting forward its views and suggestions on all civic matters. Jack Woolford was chairman for the first ten years. To commemorate the Millennium the Dover Society installed ten plaques around the town marking historic links with people and events from the past.

One of The Dover Society's ten plaques

Dover and Thanet Rights of Way Society

Dover and Thanet Rights of Way Society celebrated its 500th walk in 1999. It was founded in 1980 by Renee Parry and John Gerrard and the first walk was from St Margaret's to Kingsdown and back with 12 people. The Society now has a membership of 160 with up to 50 on its walks. Its main function is to keep rights of way open for people to enjoy the countryside with regular exercise and convivial conversation as bonuses. Guided walks of about six miles are organised on alternate Sunday mornings with a work party on the other Sundays, repairing stiles and clearing paths. All day Saturday walks with a stop for lunch are also organised.

Inaugural walk from the Dover Patrol Memorial of the Dover & Thanet Rights of Way Society in 1980

Chapter 18

MUSIC AND DRAMA

The first club formed after World War II was the Dover and District Music Club, which in fact started on the 7 May 1945 – the day before VE Day. Sydney Clout was its chairman for 20 years. After the death of his first wife he married Lillie Gambrell, Music teacher at the Girls' Grammar School. When Lillian Kay was appointed Maths mistress at the Girls' School in 1946 the Head and most of the staff were members of the new club. Lillian also joined – as was expected of her. The Town Hall used to be packed for the regular concerts including parties of pupils from Dover College and both grammar schools. It was the only club in town for a while. The subscription until 1958 was one guinea.

Miss Marguerite Laurie, a music and singing teacher, 'ruled' the committee for nearly 20 years. The club's grand piano lived in her house and went to the Town Hall when needed, although it was kept in the Town Hall permanently from 1964.

The club encouraged young and local performers and invited artists from other parts of the country, both famous names and up and coming musicians, who seemed to enjoy visiting Dover.

During the 1940s there were over 300 members but by 1953 only 130, although membership did recover to around 200 through the 1950s.

Problems began when Miss Laurie died in 1962 followed by Sydney Clout in 1964. Financial difficulties with only £100 in reserve led to concerts being held at the Girls' Grammar School rather than the Town Hall and concerts reduced from six to five a year. Despite a regular grant from Dover Council and an increase in the subscription to 35/- , in 1970 the Chairman, Archie Green, the Secretary, May Prescott and the Treasurer recommended that the club be wound up and resigned.

The club survived this trauma, however. All the officers were new and were all from the Girls' Grammar School with Lillian Kay in the chair. Five concerts were given every year until 1977 when the club reverted to six. Music was offered by local groups, schools and individual pupils. Big names were out for financial reasons. One short notice replacement was a harpist, Marisa Robles, who had to feed her baby during the interval! Alan Walker became chairman. Mrs de Vere Ashbee was involved as was Adrian Boynton, Head of Music at the Boys' Grammar, and Mary Todd, a Music teacher at the Girls' Grammar.

Despite best efforts membership continued to fall as did audiences. Charles Chitty, the Dover miller, supported the club by taking out five subscriptions until he died aged 105. Raffles and sponsorship were tried to boost funds and to supplement grants from the Council and other bodies. From 1981 a concert was shared with Dover College and the new St Mary's Parish Centre was used at a concessionary rate but there were still six concerts a year.

A big event was planned for 1982 – to go down fighting. Ian Wallace was booked for a concert and the Town Hall was packed as it had been in 1945. With a donation from Southern TV the club was 'rich'. The full Royal Marines' band was booked in 1983 at a cost of £1,000 followed by Richard Baker, the TV personality, in 1984. This proved to be the final season for the club. Despite a sizeable balance in the bank there was nobody willing to replace the retiring officers. The last concert was a full orchestral evening by a 70 strong Canterbury Orchestra and the club finally sank with colours flying.

Dover Orchestra

Sydney Clout was also the leader of the Dover Orchestra formed in 1946 by John Stainer, Music master at Dover College. Sydney Clout was followed by Ruth Jenkins (nee Burnie), a Maths mistress at the Girls'Grammar School. John Stainer was followed as conductor by Wilfrid Holland, another master at Dover College, who was also the Borough Organist until 1953 when he was succeeded

Dover Orchestra rehearsing in about 1970

by Reg Adams. Lillian Kay played viola. Ross Anderson became conductor of both the Orchestra and the Choral Society in 1960. The orchestra continued to give concerts at the Town Hall and various churches but finding conductors became a problem and by 1980 the Dover Orchestra was no more.

Dover Players

The Dover Players was formed in 1947 by Janet and Malcolm (Mac) Young. Janet was the producer and Mac was in charge of publicity and stage management. Other names from the early days were Ray Warner, Dick Massey, Ken Ruffell, Alf Gunn, Sybil Lewis, Moya Large, Lionel Bish and Bobbie Stacey. Initially they confined themselves to plays at the Town Hall like *Quiet Weekend*, *Blind Goddess*, *The Wind and the Rain* and *Book of the Month* rather than conflict with the Dover Operatic and Dramatic Society (DODS), but later they produced occasional musicals like *Salad Days* and pantomimes at the Town Hall before DODS staged them. There was no big celebration in Dover in1951 to celebrate the Festival of

Dick Massey (centre) and the cast of the Dover Players' 'On Monday Next' in 1952 including Ray Warner (second left), Bernard Harrison (standing second right), Sybil Lewis (with poodle) and Peggy Shaw next to her

Dover Players' 'Merchant of Venice' at Kearsney Abbey in 1953

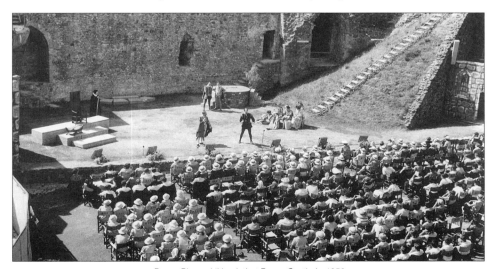

Dover Players' 'Hamlet' at Dover Castle in 1959

Britain due to a shortage of money, but there were several modest events including *A Midsummer Night's Dream* performed in the open air at Kearsney Abbey by the Dover Players and watched by 4,000 people. Jeffrey Archer (later Lord Archer), a gym master at Dover College, was a very good Puck! More open air productions at Kearsney Abbey followed: *Twelfth Night* in 1955 and *The Merchant of Venice* in Coronation year. A Shakespeare play was performed in Dover Castle in 1964 and in 1968 the Dover Players celebrated their 21st Anniversary by performing *As You Like It* at Kearsney Abbey. In danger of folding in 1969, the society revived, producing Lionel Bart's musical *Oliver* at the Town Hall and *Half a Sixpence* in 1971 but the curtain finally came down in 1973.

Dover Operatic and Dramatic Society

DODS was revived in 1950 with a production of *Iolanthe*, using a 16 inches square beam from the old Royal Hippodrome to make a proscenium for the Town

DODS' first post war production 'Iolanthe' in 1950

DODS' 'Lilac Time' 1969

Hall stage. The society traces its beginning to 1910 when a group of enthusiasts put on *HMS Pinafore* in the Town Hall as part of the Cricket Week entertainment. Encouraged by its success they formed the Dover Operatic and Dramatic Society in 1911, staging *The Mikado* in the same year. The First World War and its aftermath caused a break from 1913 until 1926 when the pattern of a musical and a play staged at either the Town Hall or the Royal Hippodrome each year resumed until 1938. Trams altered their timetables to accommodate audiences going to and from the show!

DODS adventurous *Son et Lumière* at the Castle for a month during the summer of 1961 was very successful. There was a move to have its own theatre in the 1960s and a building fund was launched and in 1971 Stanley's Mill at Temple Ewell was purchased. It was not suitable as a theatre, but did provide rehearsal rooms, scenery and costume storage and a workshop. The society celebrated its Diamond Jubilee in 1971 producing *Oklahoma* and the *Mikado*. The Pantomime Section was formed in 1975 and has produced a panto every year since. A very successful production of the musical *Annie*, starring Carly Robinson who celebrated her 11th birthday during the run was staged in 1994. Full House signs were put up at Dover Town Hall each evening as more than 2,000 people took every available seat to watch the musical. During the

DODS' 'Sound of Music' 1982. Standing from left Richard Wadey, Elizabeth Ruck, Susan Smith, Stephen Wadey and sitting John Ravenhill, Ann O'Kane, Julie Ruck, Jenny Wadey and Helen O'Kane

DODS' 1985 pantomime 'Snow White' with Kate Hibbert as Snow White

DODS' 'Oklahoma' 1986

same year the society launched The Next Generation, a new section for young people with two productions each year. At the end of the century DODS attempted to purchase the empty college premises built in 1894 in Ladywell adjoining the Town Hall, but were outbid. With five productions each year the society continues to play a major part in providing Dover's entertainment.

Karen Mennie and Steve Yarrow in DODS' 'South Pacific' 1997

Kent Music Festival

In 1951 the newly-formed Customs and Excise Waterguard Choir won two competitions at the Kent Music Festival which began before the Second World War and was held in Dover every four years using Dover College, the Town Hall and other premises on three consecutive Saturdays. Graham Tutthill recalls competing in a junior piano class when he was about 12 years old. He was one of 38 entrants who all had to play the same piece of music. Having listened to them all, the judge asked six of them to play again. After this marathon Graham was announced the winner.

Dover Pageant

1983 saw a revival of the Dover Pageant first performed in the grounds of Dover College in 1908 over several days with a cast of 2,000 and watched by thousands of people. Connaught Park was the venue in 1983 and it was staged there another seven times in the 1980s and 90s, returning to Dover College in 1999. A local hotelier, Mike McFarnell, has

Lorraine Sencicle and Michael van der Heuven in the revived Dover Pageant at Connaught Park

been 'Master of the Pageant' since 1983, working tirelessly with his team of volunteers and a cast of a couple of hundred depicting the history of Dover. Unfortunately, audiences no longer number even a thousand with so many other competing events.

The Dover Youth Theatre Project was launched in 1995 by professional actor and opera singer Marie Kelly-Thomas, giving local youngsters the chance to take part in drama and dance classes. More than 100 joined the classes in the first few weeks. In the same year young people from the Dover Music Centre were among more than 2,000 who claimed a world record by playing in the world's largest orchestra.

Dover Choral Society

The Choral Society celebrated its centenary in 1992. For its first 55 years it was known as the Choral Union but when it resumed activities after World War II it became the Choral Society in 1947. One of the driving forces behind the choir for the first 30 years was the Borough organist, H J Taylor, who was its first director. His memorial concert in 1936 featured many of his compositions including the *Dover Triumph* song, first performed in 1908.

The society is still flourishing with about 100 members under its musical director Michael Foad. Concerts are given at the Town Hall at Easter and in November every year using both professional and local soloists. The Choir also performs at the annual Come Carolling concert at the Town Hall organised by Christians Together in

Dover Choral Society Programme 1955

Dover. A regular and popular feature in recent years has been the Dover Proms concerts during Carnival Week in July when there is an open invitation for anybody to join the Prom choir. The roof of the Town Hall is raised when the traditional 'last night of the Proms' songs are sung, Union Jacks are waved and streamers 'popped'.

Miriam Knights

Choral singers in Dover said farewell in 1995 to Miss Miriam Knights when she moved to Cheltenham. She came to Dover in 1946 and taught handicrafts for 35 years at art schools in Dover and Folkestone. In her spare time Miss Knights conducted 12 different choirs during the 50 years she spent in Dover, winning over 300 awards in festivals. Among the choirs she conducted were the Dover Junior Co-op Choir, Dover Methodist Ladies' Choir and the Dover Afternoon Townswomen's Guild Choir.

The Dover Festival

The eighth Dover Festival in 1999 had a new look. The week in May started with a family fun weekend of European street theatre, the Teddy's Bear picnic in Kearsney Abbey and traditional seaside entertainment. There were five days of young people's music, dancing and drama workshops. Adults had the opportunity to take part in writing, performing and directing for the stage in Channel Theatre's 'Open Stage' programme. Other special events, the Coward and Gershwin Centenary cabarets at the Churchill Hotel, a 60s night and the Evacuees' Reunion all proved popular. Perhaps the highlight of the week was *The Dreaming Sea* performed by amateurs and professionals at Dover Castle and produced by the Strange Cargo Arts Company with impressive sculptures, haunting music, dance and special effects.

Characters

SAMUEL SHENTON

Retired Dover sign writer Samuel Shenton was convinced of one thing. The world was flat – well not quite flat – more saucer shaped. That is why he became secretary of the International Flat Earth Research Society and why the media, especially those from Fleet Street, flocked to his door. Quite often the journalists returned to London thinking perhaps there was something in what Samuel believed.

He could be quite convincing. According to him when a round-the-world yachtsman completed his circuit all the sailor had done was to navigate round the edge of the saucer-like earth. That was why yachtsmen did not fall off the end.

Samuel, back in the 1960s, gave talks in Dover to clubs and societies expounding his convictions about the saucer-shaped world. Others backed his theories and membership of his Flat Earth Society grew, he claimed, to more than 100 members worldwide.

He explained that if an untethered balloon was sent up and then brought back down to earth it would be in the same place from where it went up. How could that be if the round world was spinning on its axis?

When space travellers in Apollo 8 brought back photographs in the late 60s showing the world as a sphere many of his adherents lost faith in his belief. Even this did not shake Samuel's convictions. He was not to be swayed by such flimsy evidence. It was pretty obvious, he argued, that they were doctored photographs,

The logo of the International Flat Earth Society

probably taken in a studio. 'In some of the photographs the world looks spherical because that's the way the wide-angled camera lens distorts,' he explained at the time. With that retort he would dismiss the inquisitive and get on sorting his mail that arrived at his London Road home from all over the world.

The International Flat Earth Society still exists and its website claims that 'the known inhabited world is flat, level, a plain world.' It also recognises the work of Samuel Shenton and Lillian J Shenton.

All good things come to an end and in March 1971, aged 67, Samuel Shenton died, still refusing to believe the world was round. Dover had lost another of its characters.

Chapter 19

OTHER LEISURE PURSUITS

The people of Dover are fortunate to have a very attractive sea front, piers and cliffs to enjoy free of charge. Since the Second World War, the acquisition of additional parks and gardens have given both local people and visitors much pleasure. With the growth of television, however, commercial entertainment in Dover declined dramatically during this period. Now we have only one small struggling cinema tucked away in a side alley. Dover, once famous for allegedly having 'one pub for every day of the year' has lost many of its public houses. Dances have to use the Town Hall as do music and drama societies. We do have one or two nightclubs for the youngsters but no ten-pin bowling and no skating rink. Things were better at one time!

Parks and gardens

Before the war the only parks and gardens to enjoy were the Granville Gardens on the sea front, Connaught Park and Pencester Gardens. In 1945 the Borough Council bought the Kearsney Abbey mansion and its 25 acres for £10,000 possibly for redevelopment! Fortunately, although the mansion was, sadly, demolished leaving only the former billiard room as a tearoom, the grounds were opened to the public and are now enjoyed by thousands, particularly at the weekends. The mansion was built in 1821 by John Minet Fector, a local banker, and remained a private estate until the Second World War when it was taken over by the military. In 1970 Council plans to sell part of the Kearsney Abbey grounds for housing met violent opposition and were soon dropped.

The grounds of Kearsney Court on the opposite side of the Alkham Valley Road were acquired by Dover Rural Council in 1951, laid out as gardens and

Kearsney Abbey Mansion in 1931

opened to the public as Russell Gardens – named after a local councillor.

Dover Rotary Club provided a garden for the blind in Maison Dieu Gardens in 1954.

The high cost of maintaining pleasure grounds was a concern for Dover Council in 1954 and an investigation was launched into the cost of Connaught Park. The Council's plant nursery at Kearsney Abbey also came under fire, but it was decided that the nursery was more cost effective than buying in plants. The beautiful pre-war flower beds at Connaught Park were restored in 1957 and featured the Scouts' Jubilee. The famous whale bone arch there was removed in 1967 because it was unsafe. Connaught Park was used for various spectacular events over the years but the weather was unkind to the Dover Pageant in 1986. The Dover Lions Spectacular did better raising £4,000 for the Canterbury Pilgrims' Hospice. Annual firework displays for 5 November organised by Dover Lions have been well supported even in bad weather.

The first band concert since the war was held in Pencester Gardens in 1955. The annual visit of Forrest's Fun Fair was a popular attraction. A paddling pool was provided, but was continually vandalised until it was eventually removed. A children's skating rink was provided there in 1957, but in 1998 the space was made into a skate-boarding facility.

The Council also provided new children's playgrounds in 1957 under the Pier District viaduct and at Elms Vale, adding to those recently provided on the Buckland Estate, Union Road and Aycliffe, plus new football pitches at Elms Vale.

The presentation of new Colours to the York and Lancaster Regiment at Crabble in 1957 provided a very memorable ceremony for the 6,000 spectators. The Dover Entertainments Committee organised the town's first Navy Week in 1959 and another new event – a Whit Monday display at Crabble by girl pipers plus Beating Retreat by the Junior Leaders' Regiment Band from Old Park Barracks. Crabble Athletic Ground was also the venue for the annual military tattoo for several years.

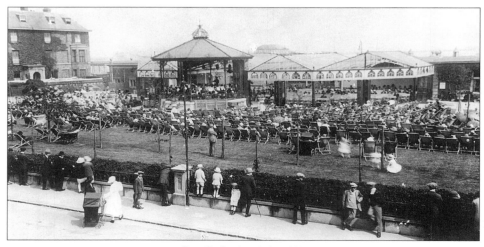

Granville Gardens in the 1920s

Granville Gardens 1957 (Dover Museum ref d02698)

In 1957 the laying out afresh of the Granville Gardens was completed and in 1961 the mosaic map in Wellesley Road and the illuminated fountain at the eastern end of the Gateway gardens made attractive additions to the sea front.

In 1974 Dover District Council, despite having no plans for its future, bought Bushy Ruff for about £90,000, comprising the colonial style house and 26 acres of gardens, the home of Mrs Constance Jorgensen. Later, in 1976, it was decided to lease the property for a country club, but planning consent was refused and an organisation was set up to protect the gardens from development. Eventually, the grounds were opened to the public as an extension to Russell Gardens and the house became a residential home for the elderly.

Cinemas

Dover's first purpose built cinema, the King's Hall in Biggin Street, which opened in 1911 but was destroyed by fire in 1937 and rebuilt in 1940, reopened in 1947 having been used as a naval training school during the war. In 1960, however, by then called the Gaumont, it closed, leaving only three cinemas in the town. They were the Odeon in London Road, the Essoldo in Cannon Street and the ABC in Castle Street. The Gaumont reopened in 1961 as a bingo hall. This pastime was becoming popular and had been played at the Co-op Hall for a few months previously. In 1968 the Essoldo Cinema, faced with falling attendances, tried wrestling and a disco

Odeon Cinema, London Road

149

Granada Cinema, later the ABC, Castle Street

club but both it and the Odeon then applied to become bingo halls leaving only the ABC in Castle Street as a cinema. The Essoldo had started life as the Plaza in 1929, converted from a bus garage! It was the scene of a brutal murder in 1941 when the manager was attacked with an axe. The Odeon finally closed in 1971 after 50 years of films on the site, first as the Buckland Picture house from 1920; renamed the Regent in 1923 it was demolished in 1936 and replaced with a new Regent, renamed Odeon after the war. The site is now a Territorial Army HQ. Dover's last cinema, the ABC, closed in 1982 and was converted into a nightclub called Images (later renamed Snoops). This cinema, opened in 1931 as the Granada, was the nation's first 'super cinema' with 1700 seats and an electronic organ. Sydney Sale was the outstanding manager from 1931 until he retired in 1957.

Dover was left without a cinema from 1982 until the Dover Museum moved back in 1991 into the refurbished Market Hall premises, bombed in 1942, with a small cinema included in the complex.

Carnivals

In 1952 the Old People's Welfare Association organised a carnival with over 40 floats, which was watched by 25,000 people and raised over £200. Earlier a fête in Russell Gardens raised £100. There was another splendid carnival in 1953 as part of the Coronation celebrations. The first ever Dover Carnival Week was held in 1956. There was varied entertainment, largely outdoor, throughout the week built around the annual Hospital Fête in Connaught Park and the carnival procession midweek. It was said that 50,000 people watched the 1960 event, which was more than the population! The RAF Red Arrows display team provided an exciting addition to the 1968 celebrations. For the first time in more than a decade, there was no carnival in 1971. The Queen's Silver Jubilee in 1977 saw a revival of the Dover Carnival after a break of seven years, a firework display, street parties and other celebrations. In the following year the Carnival Committee was able to give £1200 to three local charities.

'Dover Express' carnival float

River Methodist Church carnival float 1985

Dancing

Dancing after the war meant ballroom dancing in the 1940s and 50s with regular events at the Curzon Hall in Tower Hamlets and the Peter Street Hall, which were 'sixpenny hops.' There was also the Empress Hall on Durham Hill where the dances were a cut above those in the Co-op Hall. If you could afford 1/6 then you danced at the Town Hall but these popular Saturday night dances at the Town Hall were threatened by hooliganism and damage in 1955. New Year's Eve dances there occasionally attracted more than 1,000. 'Beat' dances for teenagers at the Town Hall arrived in the 60s but were marred by fights in 1963. By the late 60s discotheques were opening and closing at a rapid rate.

Coronation illuminated crown in Market Square 1953

The Coronation

There were street parties everywhere in 1953 to celebrate Queen Elizabeth's Coronation and the street decorations of bunting and flowers from the sea front to Buckland Bridge plus an illuminated crown in the Market Square could not be bettered anywhere in Kent. The Corporation also organised a united open air service.

Filming and television

Television became widespread during these years. Local TV reception was improved by a booster station for the BBC on the radar pylons at Swingate in

Filming 'Those Magnificent Men in Their Flying Machines' 1963. Terry Thomas extreme left

1958 and ITV began construction of a new mast at Hougham.

Dover was also a popular location for both cinema and TV films. Scenes for *Those Magnificent Men in Their Flying Machines* and *Operation Crossbow* were filmed in 1963. Film crews were in the area again in 1968 to shoot *Battle of Britain* and in 1969 for *David Copperfield*. Television crews came to Dover in 1979 to film scenes for *Telford's Change* and *Tinker, Tailor, Soldier, Spy*; BBCs *Songs of Praise* was broadcast from Dover several times. Local people were used as extras when Dover Castle was transformed temporarily into the Tower of London for a film about Lady Jane Grey.

In 1960 land at the top of Elms Vale was levelled for recreation with a new pavilion and groundsman's house. In the same year the King Charles II walk (King Charles landed at Dover in 1660 when the monarchy was restored following the Commonwealth) was opened from the sea front, under the Prince of Wales Pier to the North Pier. Sadly it disappeared when the Hoverport was built, leaving a short rump at the western end of the sea front with its commemorative plaque under a canopy. A new restaurant opened at the end of the Prince of Wales Pier with a bus service to get there if necessary! There was also a new Turret Walk on the Admiralty Pier.

Leisure Centres

Corporation plans for a swimming bath and a children's library were both halted due to the financial situation in 1961. In the same year there was a petition against the scheme for a swimming pool because of the £174,000 cost, but government economic measures postponed it anyway. The swimming pool was built at long last – at increased cost – and opened in 1972. To provide a car park for it over 300 human remains (some 300 years old) were exhumed from old St James' churchyard the following year. The sports centre was built alongside the swimming pool in 1976.

The longed for 20 lane ten-pin bowling alley on the site of Leney's Brewery was delayed by government restrictions in 1964 and Dover is still without this popular facility. In 1968, after years of resistance by the Borough Council, Dover's first amusement arcade opened in Queen Street. Now there are several in the town.

Public houses

During this period many of Dover's pubs closed or were demolished and in 1969 it was the turn of the *Prince Louis of Hesse* in Chapel Street and the *Falcon* at the Bridge St/London Road corner. Dover's oldest pub, *The Cause is Altered*, had to make way for the York Street dual carriageway in 1973 and in the same year *The Rose* in Cannon Street was converted into Abbey National offices. Others that disappeared include the *Duke of Wellington, New Endeavour, Plough, Rose & Crown, Royal Standard* and *Hand & Sceptre* all in London Road; the *Angel* in High Street; *The Salutation, Queen's Head, William IV, British Queen* and *The Wellington* in Biggin Street; *The White Lion, The Havelock Arms, The Imperial Crown* all in Tower Street; *Town Arms* in Bridge Street; *Prince of Wales* in George Street; *Sportsman* in Charlton Green; *Walmer Castle, Duchess of Kent* and *Prince*

Regent in Market Square; *Robin Hood* and *Chandos* in Townwall Street; *Invicta* and *Prince Imperial* in Snargate Street; *Archcliffe Fort* in Limekiln Street; *The Griffin* and the *Red Cow* in Folkestone Road; *Hotel de Paris* and *Swan* in Strond Street; the *New Inn* in York Street and the *Crown* in Military Road. Most of the pubs that remain were 'modernised' and the separate bars made way for a single carpeted lounge. Drink-driving laws meant that most had to offer food in order to survive as well as installing 'one-armed bandits.' Some changed their names like the *Grapes* in Maison Dieu Road becoming the *Louis Armstrong* in 1972. New pub/restaurants appeared including the *Britannia* in Townwall Street and at the end of the century the *Eight Bells* in Cannon Street.

'Five Alls Inn', Market Street

"Hotel de Paris', Strond Street

Dover Film Festival

In 1971 Ray Warner, who had by then completed his 25th annual film of Dover events, approached Ivan Green, the local historian, with the idea of a local film festival comprising a short film of general interest followed by an Ivan Green programme of 'Then and Now' slides of old Dover and concluding with Ray's annual Dover film. During the refreshment interval there would be the chance to view an exhibition provided by the Dover Museum and Library. Ian Gill, the Town Clerk, encouraged them to form a small committee to develop the idea. The committee initially consisted of just Ray and Ivan with some publicity help from Councillor Peter Bean. The first Film Festival was held in the Town Hall in 1972 and the very successful formula lasted for 27 years.

After Ray Warner's death in 1990, John Roy of River became an energetic chairman of the committee. Following his death Ron Dryden became chairman and his business acumen eased the financial situation. Phil Heath, a Dovorian and managing director of Heathfield Studios, took over the filming after Ray's death and also produced the Festival. All those involved gave their services without payment. In 1995 the Festival celebrated its 25th anniversary by presenting the only survivors of the first Festival – Margaret (Ivan's wife, projectionist and co-researcher) and Ivan Green – with a silver salver. 1997 broke all records for attendance with all five evening performances and both matinees packed. Sadly, the 1999 Festival was the last – but not for lack of public support.

Bryan Allen's man-powered flying machine 'Albatross' 1979

Son et Lumiere, which was staged for 100 evenings at the Castle in 1977 produced a debt of £36,000 with the possibility that the 18 Dover Charter Trustees (the Borough Council had disappeared with the 1974 local government reorganisation) would have to pay it themselves!

A novel event was the first man-powered flying machine to cross the Channel: Bryan Allen, a 26 year old American, pedalled the machine across in 1979 and won £100,000.

Strong feelings were aroused in 1992 when Dover District Council claimed that the increasing numbers of swans (up to almost 50) and other water fowl were creating a health hazard in Kearsney Abbey. Local protesters led by Brenda Pittaway, the voluntary swan warden, and Egham Swan Sanctuary opposed plans to reduce numbers substantially. Eventually, a fence around the lake in front of the tea room prevented most of the fowling of that area and the controversy died down.

The Channel Tunnel workings produced a unique benefit for the Dover area, creating 75 acres of new land at the bottom of Shakespeare Cliff, which was opened to the public in 1998 and named Samphire Hoe. It is managed by the White Cliffs Countryside Project and was planted with seeds from the chalk downs, which have gradually transformed the site. Walkways enable the public to enjoy the dramatic scenery of

Samphire Hoe in 1996

the chalk cliffs as well as the flora and fauna, butterflies and birds of the Hoe.

In 1998 changes were made to the layout of part of Pencester Gardens in an attempt to discourage its use by drug addicts and alcoholics. Dover Town Council marked the Millennium by building a performing arts pavilion there with a flagstone Heritage Path approach and surround. Individuals and organisations were invited to purchase flagstones, each recording a memorable event in Dover's history, at £100 each plus lettering. Unfortunately, once the Millennium Pavilion was built this became a new challenge for some skate-boarders and others. Their anti-social behaviour threatened the future of open-air concerts in this pleasant place.

Millennium Pavilion and Heritage Path, Pencester Gardens

Chapter 20

SPORT

Sydney Doble with the Olympic torch 1948

London hosted the Olympic Games in 1948 and Sidney Doble, a local runner, collected the Olympic torch from the port and ran with it through the town before handing it on.

It was a good year for sport in Dover. It was Dover FC's first professional season. Large attendances, including the 2000 strong Supporters' Club, were rewarded by the club ending seventh in the Kent League. Dover Rugby Club also had a good season winning 13 of its 21 matches. Dover Cricket Week at Crabble

County Cricket Week at Crabble

again attracted 19,000 people as in the previous year even though Kent did not win either of the two county matches! Shepherdswell won the Dover Cricket League and the Dover to London cycle race was won by T Foord in a record 2 hours 57 minutes. The Dover Table Tennis League was revived and was won by the Methodist team. The Sea Angling Association had a large membership and a record number of anglers used the Prince of Wales Pier and breakwater.

There was a strong Dover Junior Schools' Football League and in 1949 George Crickson from Astor Avenue played for England Boys. In the same year the Regatta was revived as a three day event by the Royal Cinque Ports Yacht Club.

Dover Regatta in the late 1940s

Dover FC ended up in debt in 1951 despite finishing fourth in the Kent League. Crabble Athletic Ground was well used during the winter season by Dover FC and Dover Rugby Club. Dover Ladies Hockey Club played in River Rec. Dover Athletics Club was formed during the year and several members distinguished themselves. The Connaught Basketball Club played some matches on the site of the old Granville Gardens.

1952 was a golden year for Dover FC. It won both divisions of the Kent League, the Kent Senior Cup (for the first time) and the Kent League Cup. To celebrate its centenary, Dover Cricket Club played Kent at Canterbury. The Duncannon Cup, a regular pre-war tennis competition, was revived and won by a Walmer pair. Part of

Dover Ladies' Hockey Club in the 1950s. Lillian Kay is the goalkeeper

THEY'VE GOT THE CUP AT LAST!

The big game is over, it is a Dover victory, and hundreds of supporters try to get a close-up view of the Senior Cup, as Wally McMillen is chaired by his team colleagues. Players in the picture are (left to right): Dolding, Worthington, Anderson (carrying the base), Swinfen, McMillen, Durrant, Smith and Kelly.

Dover FC first team, winners of the Kent Senior Cup, 1952. Arthur Larmer holds the cup

Kearsney Abbey was used for target practice by the newly-launched Archery Club and Dover Rowing Club did well in various regattas.

Both the Sea Angling Association and Dover Cricket Week celebrated their golden jubilees in 1953. The junior cricket knockout cup competition was in its eighth year; Cosmopolitans won the senior cricket trophy for the fifth time in eight years and the Co-op won the Division II Cup. All the local bowling clubs: Dover, Kearsney, River and Buckland Mill did well. In football Dover Wanderers won Group A of the Kent Junior Cup and River Sports won Group B. Dover FC was runner up in the Kent League. Sadly, Dover Sailing Club was wound up, unable to find new premises following demolition of its Liverpool Street HQ.

Dover Rowers won all three County championships in 1956 for

Fishing from the breakwater in the 1940s

the first time since 1921. A Dover schoolboys' football team reached the divisional final of the English Schools Shield played at Crabble in front of 2000 spectators. A.B. Taylor, a Dover headmaster and keen supporter of school football, retired during the year. He had been Chairman of the English Schools Football Association. Dover hosted the Kent Amateur Athletics Championships at Crabble for the first time in 1956.

Dover FC did well in 1957 but attendances were poor and the club was only kept afloat by the efforts of the Supporters' Association. Dover Boys also did well sharing the Kent Schools' Fletcher Football Cup. They won 11 titles in the Kent Boys Boxing Championships with five boys reaching the regional finals of the English Schools Championships. Two of the boys made it to the semi-finals but Danny Da Costa from the Boys' Grammar lost in the final. The Rugby Club had its best season for 20 years.

Dover Judo Club was formed in 1958. Schoolboy boxers again did well and eight local scholars took part in the All England Schools Athletics Championships with Diane Sawyer (later to become mayor as Diane Smallwood) of Whitfield winning the high jump. The Duke of York's Royal Military School won the Kent Boys' Swimming Championships and the Kent long distance swimming championships were held in Dover Harbour. Dover Athletics Club started an annual contest with Calais and a new boxing club, Jasper House, met at the Working Men's Club.

The Kent Football League died in 1959 with few mourners. Dover and seven other clubs joined the Southern League. Dover was on the brink of financial disaster, but a new supporters' association attracted 10,000 members in three months. Fred Durrant, manager for ten seasons resigned and Alex McCue took over, winning more games and more support. During the following season Dover was in the first round proper of the FA Cup for the first time and won the Kent Senior Cup for the first time in ten years. A combined Dover tennis team played Nore Navy Command during Dover's Navy Week.

In 1960 there was a rapid growth in Sunday soccer and the Junior Leaders' Regiment won both the Boys' Army soccer and boxing cups.

After only 18 months Alex McCue left Dover FC and was succeeded in 1961 by Pat Beasley, an ex-Arsenal footballer. Floodlights were installed at the ground but results on the pitch were poor. The Dover Junior Football League celebrated its golden jubilee; Frank Turner had been secretary for 30 years. Dover Amateur Boxing Club had success at both county and national level and Ray Robinson was selected for England against Germany. The Dover Home Guard (1944) Rifle Club closed after its range in the Trevanion Street caves was flooded, but members were able to join the Dover Rifle Club. Despite attendances of 10,000, Dover Cricket Week was threatened due to rising costs. Dover and District Tennis League, which had been running for over ten years, had a very successful year. Mrs Kremer and Mrs Saunders were the ladies' doubles champions with A.R. Jackson and Harry Smith the men's champions. Greenleas Tennis Club won the mixed and doubles league. In 1961 Dover Swimming Club, founded in 1886, merged with Dover Lifeguards, founded in 1935. The club's main purpose was to teach people to swim and life save but also to coach for long distance swimming. In 1977 its hut on the beach was replaced by a new beach headquarters and by the end of the century the club boasted 400 members and a full-time coach.

Dover FC held on to the Kent Senior Cup in 1962 and in the Dover and District Junior Football League the Borstal boys won the First Division. Dover Rugby Club had its best ever season fielding four teams every week. New dressing rooms were provided at Elms Vale in 1963. In the same year the former Grand Shaft Barracks gymnasium on the Western Heights opened as a council sports centre and was used by the popular 5-a-side Football League.

1964 was a turbulent year for Dover FC. Manager Pat Beasley left after three years and Roy Little from Crystal Palace took over. Only six of the 21 players were retained! Club Chairman Len Clarke resigned and fans dropped by half. Things were not much better in the following year with players coming and going and the club still losing money. Other sports were more successful: Dover Hockey Club's two teams lost only one match; the Judo Club did well in national competitions; the Darts League gained new teams and the Dover Go-Kart Club was competing all over the south of England. In cricket Colin Cowdrey carried his bat at Dover with 99 not out. This performance was dampened by Leslie Ames, the Kent secretary, announcing that there would be only one county game at Dover in 1966 because of the poor state of the wicket.

There was trouble for local tennis in 1966 over complaints about the annual doubles tournament held at the Connaught Club. Phil Peirce, the League Secretary since it was formed 15 years previously, resigned. The league continued but without the Immigration and Customs teams. Phil Peirce resumed as secretary and was presented with a league badge at the AGM, normally only given to league match players. Tennis clubs were having difficulty maintaining membership but over 30 youngsters received coaching each year in Dover under a Kent Junior Coaching Scheme run by Phil Peirce for several years and then by Sheila Stewart.

In 1966 three Castlemount boys were in a Kent team, which won the British Schools' Judo Competition. Dover Ladies' Hockey Club was revived. Dover FC changed managers again when Jack Clover – ex Grenadier Guards sergeant-major – took over and the team won 15 games in succession taking it to the top of Division 1 of the Southern League for several months. This tremendous turnabout was achieved without new players.

Thirteen Dover FC players left in 1969 including player/manager Bill Swain. The men's section of Dover Hockey Club folded in 1970 although the women's section was still thriving.

In 1971 there was no county cricket at Crabble due to the state of the wicket; the Council agreed to send the head groundsman on a wicket preparation course and one county match was allocated to Dover the following year when the wicket was perfect, the sun shone for three days and Cowdrey scored a century! Dover FC won the Kent Senior Cup again in 1971 but by 1973 spectators were averaging only 650 per match. Dover Athletics Club was newly formed in 1972.

Dover and Deal Sports Councils merged in 1974 to become Dover & District in line with local government reorganisation. In the county cricket match Cowdrey scored 119 and Underwood took 6 wickets for 42 runs, but the wicket was criticised again; after more work it was given the all clear once more. Dover & District Bar Billiards League was formed in the same year. Both Lydden and

Coombe Valley racing circuits were popular with car and motorbike racing enthusiasts.

1975 was a notable year for local sport. Watersports were doing well with Dover Rowing Club taking part in the Thames Head of the River Race for the first time; the Royal Cinque Ports Yacht Club and the Ramsgate, Calais and Boulogne clubs inaugurated a new series of cross Channel races called 'Challenge du Channel.' The Bushido Society was so popular that it was looking for larger premises. Dover Rangers won the Dover Charities Cricket Knockout Competition for the eighth time in nine years. With county cricket at Crabble again under threat, Dover District Council gave £350 to save it for one more year. Dover Rugby Club celebrated its golden jubilee by playing a Kent XV. Dover Squash Club was formed and table tennis, after some lean years, was making a come back. Dover FC reached the second round of the FA Cup for the first time. Admission charges went up from 35p to 45p!

At long last the £300,000 Sports Centre, next to the swimming pool, was opened in 1976 by Dover District Council Chairman, Peter Bean. Its first manager was Harry Croxton from Liverpool. Very soon several new clubs were operating there. A Dover Summer Bowls League was formed and the Sea Angling Association members built and opened their own HQ in Priory Road. Dover & District Junior Football League honoured Bill Wright and Bill Newell who had 80 years service between them. Tommy Coulter who had succeeded Terry Adlington as the Dover FC manager in 1975 was sacked and replaced by Alf Bentley with the club £7,000 in debt. The annual Dover-Calais Festival of Sport, held in Dover with 500 competitors was won by Dover. The local Sunday Football League could now boast 36 teams compared with seven only three years previously. Dover & District Tennis League with its veteran chairman, Cecil Wright, celebrated 25 years with a special tournament at Connaught Park. 122 crews entered Dover Rowing Club's annual regatta in the harbour.

Due to the state of the wicket there was again no county cricket in 1977. Except for this it was another great year for local sport. David Wilkie, the Olympic gold medallist, opened the Lifeguards new HQ on the beach and Dover's England darts player, Tony Brown, won the British open pairs title. Mike Bell of Dover Squash Club won a national event and Lydden-based speedway star, Ted Hubbard, rode for England against Australia at Canterbury and was top scorer. Dover Volleyball Club won the Folkestone League and Dover Badminton Club won the East Kent League men's, ladies and mixed doubles. To cap it all, Dover FC was undefeated at home in 21 games. In addition Dover District Bowling League, Dover Squash League and Dover Pub Pool League – the first in Kent – all started.

Dover won the Kent Super Darts League in 1978 but Dover FC was relegated from the First Division South of the Southern League. Dover Schools' cricket captain, Chris Penn, played for England boys twice. The fifth Kent Festival of Sport was held in Dover with 30 sports at 17 venues.

In 1980 the 'Dover Darlins,' a female promotions team, attempted to boost Dover FC's lottery and Paul Marklew windsurfed across the Channel.

Dover Cricket Club won the Kent Cricket League in 1981 and hundreds of competitors in Dover's first 10 mile fun run raised £1,000; 600 took part the following year. In the same year Dover Road Runners Club organised a 78 miles run from London to Dover and raised £500 for dependents of British casualties in the Falklands War.

1982 was another bad year for Dover FC: Manager Peter Brooks was sacked and the club could not afford to pay some players – several left. Other sports were more fortunate: Dover & District Premier Pigeon Club won top honours at the Kent Cosmopolitan Federation dinner; Dover & District Skittle Association had 88 teams, a record number; Andrew Hayes, aged 14, of Dover Boxing Club won the National Schools' Amateur Boxing Association title, but the club itself had an internal disagreement which led to several resignations including Arthur Spratling who had founded the club 32 years previously. Dover Charity Darts League presented Buckland Hospital with £1,000 raised during the winter. The Dover & District Cricket League was formed, Chris Penn made his debut for Kent and Dover Boys' Grammar pupil, Richard Pepper aged 17, was selected for the England Schools' under 19 cricket team – brother Stuart, aged 16, was chosen for Kent's under 17 tour. Dover Bowling Club celebrated its 75th birthday. Bill Solly, Chairman of the Sea Angling Association, led England to victory over Eire and the Crabble Pavilion, renovated at a cost of £120,000, was officially opened.

Dover FC reached rock bottom in 1983 when it was compulsorily wound up owing £80,000. A group of businessmen, headed by John Husk, came to the rescue and leased the Crabble ground, formed a new team called Dover Athletic and appointed Alan Jones, a former Dover player, as manager. Dover Table Tennis Association celebrated its 50th anniversary and Michael Rutherford, aged 12 from Astor, was selected for the England Schools' Table Tennis Team. Dover Rowing Club's Roger Cuff was manager of the UK dragon boat racing team. Alan Clark, aged 64, Dover Rangers' football secretary, received Kent County FA's long and meritorious award for 40 years service. Dover won the Dover-Calais Sports Festival for the first time since 1976. Dover's cricketer, Derek Aslett, was in great form for Kent and was awarded his county cap. Playing for England's Schools, Richard Pepper won an award for outstanding fielding. The Sea Angling Association provided two England captains during the year – Alan Yates and Bill Solly. Kearsney Bowling Club produced its youngest ever champion, Jeff Vane aged 24, who had only been playing for five years. RCPYC'S Nick and Tony Smither became the World Hornet champions.

In 1984 there were 50 different sports groups in the area. The Boxing Club produced a national schoolboys' champion in 16 year old Andrew Hayes. The biggest motorcycle grass track event ever seen in England was at Lydden Circuit when it staged the

Jeff Vane, aged 24, Kearsney Bowling Club's youngest-ever champion, 1983

European championships. Dover Primary Schools' football team had its best season ever winning 20 of its 24 matches and Crabble hosted a touring Australian ladies' cricket team who played a Kent side. Alan Jones left Dover Athletic and was replaced by Steve McRaye; he was replaced a year later by Chris Kinnear. The Junior Leaders' Regiment won for the sixth successive year the Junior Army Under 20s individual and team fencing championships and Emma Langton won the English Schools' junior 800 metres championship. Crabble hosted a cricket match between the 1970 Kent side and a 1985 Kent Side.

Dover's Sports Aid raised £7,000 for Africa in 1986 with hundreds of people running. A massive increase in sports charges by the Council brought a wave of protests and the Sports Centre, in dire straits from falling attendances, installed a giant waterslide as a new attraction. Lyndon Dunsbee, aged 17 of Dover Lifeguards, was named British Long Distance Swimmer of the Year. In the same year he, Bridget Young and Richard Davey swam for England in long distance events. Schoolgirl athlete Emma Langton won her first international race. Kearsney Bowling Club celebrated its 80th birthday. Dover mechanic Darren Dixon of Coombe Valley Motorcycles won a major international event and Bernard Downs of Dover Rifle Club (formed in 1900) was successful in the British championships. The Sea Angling Association celebrated the Diamond Jubilee of its Pier Fishing Festival and during the year there was a dramatic rescue of 158 fishermen from the breakwater who were at risk of being trapped by a strong gale.

Allan Edgington, lifelong member of the Sea Angling Association with a 10.5lb bass

In 1987 Dover District Council, concerned about the cost of maintaining its sports facilities, invited sports clubs to discuss taking over the maintenance of council-owned pitches and pavilions, but met only criticism. In the following year the District Council threatened to sell off River Recreation Ground for housing, but it was saved by the newly-formed River Parish Council purchasing it. Still in 1987, Karen Seal, aged 17 of Dover Lifeguards, was selected for the Great Britain youth squad and Darren Byer was voted British Long Distance Swimmer of the Year. It was the year of the *Herald of Free Enterprise* disaster and Dover Rugby Club played a side from the visiting *HMS Illustrious* to raise money for the disaster fund. Bernard Down and Mike West of Dover Rifle Club were in the British national squad. Dover Rangers Sports Club celebrated 50 years but the Dover Charities Cricket Knockout Competition was wound up.

Dover Athletic ended the 1989-90 season at the top of the Premier Division and was all set for promotion to the Vauxhall Conference, but this was refused because the ground was not up to standard.

Dover Rugby Club played 'HMS Illustrious' in aid of the 'Herald of Free Enterprise' disaster fund, 1987

Sarah Marsh, 17, retained her English ladies' light-weight kickboxing title in 1994 but the big event of the year was the start in Dover of the Kent stage of the Tour de France cycling race through the streets of Dover. The pavements and vantage points were thronged with thousands of people waiting for the cyclists who flashed by in a couple of minutes! Dover Harbour Board's (DHB) plans for a new watersports centre on the beach in front of the

Dover Athletic, Beazer Homes Premier Division Champions again, 1992/93. Steve Warner and Colin Blewden are holding the shield
(Dover Museum ref d24872)

Tour de France cyclists in Folkestone Road, 1994 (Dover Museum ref d22955)

Granville Gardens proved very controversial and planning permission was eventually refused.

Suggestions in 1995 that the former Old Park Barracks site at Whitfield could be turned into a major sports centre came to nothing. In the same year Dover had a national full-contact karate champion when Stewart Edmonds won the heavyweight title. Dover Rowing Club celebrated its 150th anniversary in 1996.

The Dover Sea Angling Association built a new restaurant, banqueting and entertainment centre in Snargate Street called Bluebirds, which opened in 1996. This popular association, boasting some 700 anglers and 750 social club members, was formed in 1903, but was interrupted by the Second World War; although it lost no time resuming – on 18 May, 1945. Its headquarters at the Clock Tower were replaced in 1976 by larger premises in Priory Road. Perhaps its biggest challenge came in 1987 when the hurricane damaged Admiralty Pier, rendering it unsafe for fishermen. Following contractual negotiations with DHB, half the pier was reopened in 1989 and the other half, repaired by members, was reopened in 1992. The association now runs the Admiralty Pier walk under licence from DHB. With frequent social functions, fishing from the Breakwater and at least 60 angling competitions a year the association is as popular as ever. Dover was chosen as the venue for the 1997 World Shore Sea Angling Championships.

In 1997 Grammar School girl Charlotte Niblett had an important week competing in the Commonwealth Games and waiting for her GCSE results. In 1997 River Originals Tennis Club celebrated 50 years with a reunion dinner. Two of its founder members were Hilda and Cecil Wright who also founded the Dover & District Tennis League and worked tirelessly for both River and the League for many years. Cecil played at the net in doubles although hardly tall enough to see over it! In the twenty years after the war there were many tennis clubs in the area including Seeboard, Young Teachers, Dover Harbour Board, Post Office, Co-op, Barwicks, NALGO, The Ramblers, Connaught, Customs, Immigration and Greenleas. By the end of the century River Originals was the only tennis club.

Dover schoolgirl, Carly Burton, continued to do well at sport in 1998, finishing third in the senior girls' discus event at the English Schools championships.

Mr Price, President of the Dover & District Tennis League, presenting trophies to representatives of River Originals Tennis Club (Cecil Wright on the far right)

August 1998 brought nautical fever to Dover as the new look regatta, initiated by Dover Town Council, involved a range of water activities including dragon-boat racing. Between races the spectators browsed amongst the sea front stalls including several from Calais and enjoyed themselves on the fairground rides.

So ended 50 years of very varied activity, involving thousands of participants and with many outstanding achievements by Dover's sportsmen and women.

Characters

FRED HAMMOND

On virtually any day of the year on the sea front around 10am Fred Hammond can be seen taking his daily swim in the harbour using his perfect crawl stroke. Fred is well known to Channel swimmers the world over.

He was born in Last Lane in 1921 and attended St Mary's Boys' School in Queen Street where every boy was expected to learn to swim. In 1935 Fred swam for the school and for Dover on the same evening at the Salt Water Baths on the sea front.

Money was scarce. Fred and his childhood friends would earn pennies whenever the opportunity arose. During the school summer holidays the harbour would be full of yachts and their owners would come ashore to shop. Boys would look after their dinghies for 6d or even a shilling. On summer Sundays they would make pictures in the sand on the east side of the jetty opposite Douro Place called the Nib or Ping Pong for some reason. The sand pictures would be made from chalk, pebbles and seaweed and promenaders would throw pennies. Fred always made the same picture, the racing yacht Shamrock that had won the America's Cup. He had to help his father who had a fruit and vegetable stall in the Market Hall. Father also sold wild rabbits and if they went mouldy Fred would have to skin them and take the pelts to Castle's in Peter Street where he would get 4d each for them. The regatta was no holiday for Fred. No stalls were allowed on the sea front until after midnight on the first day of the regatta. Before he was 12, Fred would have to be behind the yacht club at midnight. When twelve struck from the clock tower he would have to push three barrow stalls into the best positions. During the regatta his job was to collect the takings from the men

Fred, Beachmaster

manning his father's stalls using a half bushel box in the carrier of his bicycle! Fruit, balloons, toffee apples, paper hats, drinks, blowers, toy monkeys on elastic balls, confetti and roasted peanuts were sold. Lots of confetti was sold because the lads used to stuff it down girls' blouses and then shake them until it emerged from the other end! Father would buy five hundred weight of peanuts and get them roasted by the baker on Durham Hill.

When Fred left school he worked for his father, Ted, but he ran away when he was 15, tired of delivering orders on his bicycle to St Margaret's or collecting a crate of raspberries from Tilmanstone. After a spell in a London dry cleaning firm he returned to Dover in 1938 and worked on Southern Railway's ferries where the crew had to provide their own bedding as well as their own food and cook it. Somehow, the captain always knew when the Customs rummage crew was going to board, giving the crew time to throw contraband out of the portholes.

At the outbreak of war in 1939 Fred was working on the *Isle of Thanet*, which was converted into a hospital ship, sailing to Dunkirk twice during the evacuation. After a spell ferrying troops on the Stranraer crossing to Ireland, he joined a succession of tramp steamers plodding to and fro the Atlantic in convoy, before entering the Royal Navy in 1944. He remembers being in the Paramount Theatre in New York in 1942 and hearing the song *White Cliffs of Dover* for the first time, sung by Connie Boswell one of the three Boswell Sisters. He was on the first ship to enter Boulogne after its liberation, carrying stores for Canadians. Despite his life at sea Fred managed to court a Wren working in the Castle caves and they married as soon as the war ended.

After 1945 Fred earned a living collecting scrap metal in a small lorry. His father bought the interior of the old Hippodrome for its scrap metal and also sold the seats all over Kent. Access was via the stage door at the rear using a ladder and Dad entered, in the dark, found himself on the stage and promptly fell into the orchestra pit! During lunch breaks the work gang would 'do a turn' on the stage. Fred also helped Dad in the fruit and vegetable business driving every night to Spitalfields Market to arrive by 5am. Crops of several orchards would be bought in advance and would then have to be picked and sold. Permission was obtained from the military to collect the wild cabbage that grows on the cliffs between Deal and Folkestone Warren. This would be taken to Spitalfields every two days. Fred still eats some every winter making sure to avoid the bitter purple version.

In 1955 he took over the Market Hall business from his father and had to move with the other stall holders to the empty Hattons premises. When everybody was evicted from Hattons, Fred closed the business and returned to working on the ferries as quarter master with Townsend-Thoresen from 1975 until he retired in 1986.

The sea has been Fred's main source of leisure all his life, swimming, sailing and water-skiing. Soon after the war he acquired what was left of a Snipe sailing dinghy and restored it, winning the 1950 Dover Regatta races. He and Maurice Sayer bought an Essex I design and won a bronze medal in the 1951 Regatta. Fred also joined the re-formed Dover Swimming Club using a pillbox on the sea front for changing. Water polo was another interest and Fred refereed matches all over Kent and London. He was also a member of Whitstable and Seasalter Water-

Ski Club and celebrated his 50th birthday by water-skiing from Dover to Calais in 1 hour and 5 minutes.

By the mid 1950s Fred was training cross Channel swimmers. His first was Jimmy Grainger of Dover Swimming Club. During night training for the 1956 Butlin's race Fred took a bucketful of jellyfish with him and threw them over the side in front of the swimmer to accustom him to jellyfish! He also joined the committee of the Channel Swimming Association and was made a life member. Swimmers from all over the world used to visit his fruit stall for supplies. Following his retirement in 1986, he has maintained a daily routine of a morning swim in the harbour throughout the year. During the summer months, swimmers from all over the world come to him on the beach for advice on swimming the Channel.

About five years ago an Australian doctor asked Fred what sort of Channel swimmer he was and Fred replied, 'You're a 12 hour swimmer.' After successfully completing his swim Dr Hinchcliff told Fred that he was mistaken as it had only taken him 11 hours 59 minutes!

Fred with Dr Hinchcliff

Fred with Molly Williams and Alison Streeter after her 32nd crossing in 1995

Fred also acts as unofficial 'beachmaster' making sure that pebble throwing does not endanger swimmers, clearing litter and keeping dogs off the beach. If you have time to spare Fred will tell you a hundred and one amusing incidents from his fascinating life!

Chapter 21

CHANNEL SWIMMING

Dover and the 21 mile sea crossing to France remains the mecca of marathon swimming. When Matthew Webb made his pioneer swim of the Dover Strait in 1875 many claimed nobody else would ever follow his example, but swimmers from all over the world have tried to emulate his feat. More and more are doing so successfully.

From 1950 to the turn of the century more than 800 men, women and young people successfully completed such swims, making a total in the 125 years since Captain Webb of 835 solo successes accepted by the Channel Swimming Association (CSA). This includes 23 two-way swims and 3 three-way crossings by solo swimmers.

A relatively new craze is swimming the English Channel in relay and in the years 1950-2000 there were more than 300 such successes recognised by the association including 30 two-way crossings, 2 three-way crossings and even one four-way crossing. By

Matthew Webb statue, Dover sea front

1986 3,700 attempts had been made on the Channel. Stronger and fitter swimmers, aided by the improved knowledge of the pilots and more accurate weather forecasts, have proved those early doubters very wrong.

Virtually every year, in the half century under review, speed records were broken. Other swimmers claimed to be the youngest, oldest, most handicapped and so on. The youngest was Tom Gregory, aged 11, who swam from France to Dover in 1988. The oldest was Clifford Batt from Australia, who was 67 when he took 18 hours 15 minutes in 1987. In 1961 came the first 'there and back' success of Antonio Abertondo, 42, from Argentina with a time of 43 hours 10 minutes. After swimming from Shakespeare Beach to France, he took four minutes to stretch his legs ashore and then swam back, taking 12 agonising hours over the last six miles. It was estimated that the ordeal would shorten his life by 20 years! Twenty years later came the first three way swim by Jon Erikson (USA) in 38 hours 27 minutes. The same year, 1961, saw Dover-born Rosemary George, 22,

Ted Erikson (USA) completes the 2nd two-way swim after 30 hours 3 minutes in 1965

become the first 'home grown' person to be successful. 1999 brought the first successful relay swim by naturists!

There is friendly rivalry over who can swim the Channel the most times. It is thought that just 35 swimmers have made 30% of all Channel crossings. Alison Streeter, 'Queen of the Channel' in the 50 year time frame, swam the Channel 39 times, CSA chairman Mike Read and journalist Kevin Murphy 32 each. Alison set other records, too. She became the fastest woman to swim from France to England in 1988 (8 hours 48

Alison Streeter celebrates her 32nd world record Channel swim in 1995

minutes) and in 1990 was the first woman to complete a three way swim (34 hours 40 minutes). With seven successful swims in 1992, she set a new record for the most cross Channel swims in one year. Alison has also raised a lot of money for charity and was awarded the MBE.

Publicity-wise the highlights in Channel swimming came in the series of international races organised by the *Daily Mail*, the first in 1950 with 24 starters, then by Butlins in 1955 and in 1975 the start of a series of races organised by the Saudi Arabian Swimming Federation. In those days thousands of spectators crowded Shakespeare Beach and other places to see the swimmers. These days onlookers can only see them depart because in 1993 the French authorities banned the start of swims from their side of the English Channel.

As more and more swimmers succeeded the public's interest in the sport waned with hardly ever a mention in the national media, except when things went wrong. Renata Agondi, 25, died while making her attempt to swim from Dover to France. Since the sport began there have been three fatalities. The first was Ted May, 44, father of nine from Scunthorpe, who refused to take an escort boat. His body was washed up on the Dutch coast in 1954. In 1999 Fausta Marin Moreno (Mexico) became the third.

Sam Rockett – first Briton ashore in the 1950 Daily Mail race

(Dover Museum ref d02829)

Ever since 1927 the recognised 'watchdog' of the sport has been the Channel Swimming Association, which tries to put an observer on every attempt or makes every effort to validate a successful claim, but in 1998 a rift resulted in Mike Oram, the one-time secretary of the CSA, breaking away and forming his own association, the Channel Swimming & Piloting Association, based at Ramsgate, to certify successful Channel swims. The schism caused considerable bitterness.

The familiar sight in Dover Harbour throughout the summer of Channel hopefuls swimming across the harbour for up to six hours at a time as they train for their expensive ordeal seems set to continue. This challenge is commemorated on the sea front by modern sculptures of two Channel swimmers.

Promenade sculptures

Chapter 22

GENERAL ELECTIONS

The Dover Parliamentary Constituency, once a safe Conservative seat, proved to be a marginal in the second half of the 20th century.

Pre-war Major Astor (Conservative) won most general elections and by October 1931 reached the peak of his popularity with a majority over Labour of 19,962.

At the end of the 1939-45 war, when the country swung to the left, J.R.Thomas (Labour) beat John Arbuthnot (Conservative) by 1,682 votes. There were only the two candidates. In 1950 Dover swung to the right with John Arbuthnot beating Charles Owen (Labour) by 2,309 votes. There were four candidates with the Communist, Bob Morrison, polling only 474 votes. A year later, John Arbuthnot again beat Charles Owen, this time by 3,516 votes. There were just two candidates. John Arbuthnot defended his seat against Jack Lee (Labour) successfully in 1955 with a majority of 3,018 and in 1959 with a 3,241 majority.

By 1964 the country was swinging left again and David Ennals (Labour) captured Sir John Arbuthnot's seat with a slender majority of 418 votes. The third candidate, a Liberal, received 5,843 votes. David Ennals boosted his majority to 3,616 in the next election in 1966 over journalist Tom Stacey (Conservative) with barrister Bernard Budd (Liberal) receiving 3,981 votes.

John Arbuthnot celebrates his win in 1950

In June 1970 there was another swing, this time to the right, when barrister Peter Rees (Conservative) captured the seat from David Ennals with a majority of 1,649. Although there were only two candidates there was an amazing turnout of electors of 80%. February 1974 saw another election with four candidates when Peter Rees retained his seat with a majority of 4,850. His opponents were Len Bishop (Labour), pub landlord Bill Stone (Independent) and Scot Young (Liberal). The turnout was 84.5%. Later the same year, in October 1974, Peter Rees once again held on to his seat with a majority over Labour of 2,294. His opponents were Len Bishop and businessman Scot Young.

David Ennals (second left) captures the seat from John Arbuthnot (right) in 1964

Left to right: Dorothy Bushell, Edmund Bushell (Mayor), Harold Wilson (Prime Minister), David Ennals MP, Councillor Cyril Chilton

There were five candidates in the May 1979 general election and once again Peter Rees was the victor with a majority of 7,942. Opposition came from Jane Chapman (Labour), dental surgeon Jack Cohen (Liberal), port worker Jeremy Fox (Silly Party) and Paul Johnson (National Front). The Silly Party received nearly twice as many votes as the National Front. Peter Rees was re-elected yet again in June 1983, this time with a 9,220 majority. There were four candidates including one from the Ecology Party polling 404 votes. The turnout was 77.65%.

By June 1987 the Conservatives had a different candidate but company director David Shaw (Conservative) was the winner with a 6,541 majority. Turnout was 79.8% with three candidates. Never had there been so many candidates as in April

Peter Rees (left) visiting the port in 1980

1992 when seven sought election. David Shaw (Conservative) retained his seat but his majority was down to 833. River resident Gwyn Prosser, a former ferry officer, represented Labour for the first time. The other candidates were Colin Percy (Natural Law with 127 votes), archaeologist Brian Philp (Independent Conservative with 250 votes), Dover solicitor Peter Sherred (Independent with 407 votes), Michael Sole (Liberal Democrat with 6,212 votes) and Adrian Sullivan (Green Party with 637 votes). The turnout was 83.6%.

There was another swing in May 1997 when, as part of the national Labour landslide victory, Gwyn Prosser (Labour) with 29,535 votes ousted David Shaw (Conservative) who received

David Shaw

Gwyn Prosser

17,796 votes. Other candidates were Mark Corney (Liberal Democrat with 4,302 votes), Susan Anderson (Referendum Party with 2,124 votes) and retired headmaster Clive Hyde of Whitfield (UK Independence Party with 443 votes). Labour's victory nationally put Tony Blair into Downing Street, the youngest prime minister for nearly 200 years. Mr Shaw did not stand for election in Dover again and his unsuccessful Conservative successor at the next election was Paul Watkins, a former nurse and District Councillor from Deal.

Characters

FREDDIE OVERTON

Dover's most flamboyant character in the second half of the 20th century must have been dancing teacher Freddie Overton. Born of humble parents in Deal in 1904, he strutted around Dover after enjoying the good life on the Riviera with some of the wealthiest women in Europe.

He was determined to be mayor of Dover but never succeeded, despite officially proposing himself for that post. Champagne-drinking Freddie was never slow in putting himself forward. 'I have lived a fabulous life with hardly any money in my pocket,' was one of his many boasts.

During his life he had a variety of jobs including being a grinder at Dover Engineering Works, tea boy at Dover Harbour station, a clerk for seven years at Chitty's Mill at Charlton Green, odd job man and conveyor belt operator at the Channel Tunnel works and a member of the professional dancing team at Hammersmith Palais. He started teaching dancing in 1924. Just before Hitler's armies marched all over Europe, from 1935-1939 Freddie was the professional host at Bobby's in Folkestone. Ladies could hire his dancing services at a shilling a time. There were always doubts about Freddy's sexual preference but in the days when homosexual activities were illegal, that was not a question one asked him.

He did say in 1974, 'When I left home in 1931 my mother thought dancing immoral and predicted that my dancing would take me down to the gutter. It was that sort of comment that made me decide never to marry. I think women are cold, calculating and callous.' Yet Freddie admitted he lived well, on the French and Italian Rivieras and other places, at the expense of wealthy women whom he accompanied as a dancing partner. 'In those days before World War II there were many beautiful, exciting, gracious women who were willing to pay for my services. Many are the stories I could tell about what went on. Why, some even tried to seduce me,' Freddie said.

He was delighted when he was elected a member of Dover Borough Council serving for nine

Freddie Overton

years, even more so when appointed an alderman for six years, but the mayoralty never came his way – his greatest regret. He was always a rebel in the council chamber. He formed a ratepayers' association and kept up a barrage of letters criticising the council and others in the local newspaper.

He organised Dover's first post-war carnival procession, dressed as a cowboy, ran Dover's American Square Dance Club and was co-founder of the Dover Hoteliers Association. Many remember Freddie best for the wartime dances, often under shellfire, at the Town Hall when the floor was packed with soldiers, sailors and airmen. At least one former Dover mayor met her husband-to-be there. Freddie was an official observer for the Channel Swimming Association but could not swim and was President of Dover Cage Bird Society, without ever keeping a cage bird in his life; he was also Vice-President of the national Music Users Council – only because 'I'm a bloody good fiddler.'

Freddie's good life had to come to an end sometime and he died in 1991.

Chapter 23

THE MILLENNIUM

This review of the last 55 years of the 20th century in Dover ends with the celebration of the Millennium when the town excelled itself to welcome the next thousand years.

Peacelight procession to the sea front 31 December 1999

Carnival of the Planets procession 1 January 2000

For thousands of Dovorians and many visitors to the town, the highlight must have been the celebrations on the sea front. They started on 31 December 1999 with a service attended by about 500 people, organised by Christians Together in Dover, in the grounds of Dover College where a thousand years before monks worshipped. This was followed by a 'home-made' peacelight lantern procession, in which hundreds joined, accompanied by a street band through the town centre, to the sea front while church bells rang out. On the packed sea front 5,000 people watched a 30 foot high sculpture of the Clock of the Second Millennium tick away its final moments on the beach before bursting into flames accompanied by spectacular fireworks. It was a night not to be forgotten.

Well in advance, it was known throughout the country that the first place to witness the dawn of the new century in Britain would be the South Foreland at St Margaret's Bay. The authorities feared the roads leading to the Bay would be overwhelmed with visitors and that crowds could easily go over the cliffs. Plans were made to seal off the village, but the fears were groundless; although a number went to the cliff top to see the dawn, there was no need to implement the cordon plan.

In Dover on 1 January 2000 there were dawn Christian services on the sea front and the cliffs to welcome the 2000th anniversary of the birth of Christ.

The crowds returned to the town centre the following evening when the new Millennium was welcomed in with the Carnival of Planets, a spectacular mardi-gras style community carnival parade that assembled in Dover College and made its way to the sea front. 300 participants wore fantastic costumes that they had spent many hours creating in workshops held throughout the district. On the beach was the Clock of the Third Millennium, which was set in motion by a climax of sound and pyrotechnics watched by an estimated 12,000 people. A fabulous firework display from Dover Castle rounded off the evening.

Many organisations made their own contribution to celebrate the Millennium, assisted by Dover District Council, which spent £1.3 million in special grants. The Dover Society decided to erect ten blue plaques around the town marking buildings and places of historic interest. Trees were planted including a yew at Dover Castle and an icon representing the Millennium was placed in the chapel

Guild of St Helena planting a yew tree sapling by St Mary-in-Castro

of St Mary in Castro. In Dover a Heritage Path was created by the town council around the performing arts pavilion in Pencester Gardens.

The year 2000 ended quietly even though it could be argued that 31 December 2000 was really the end of the Second Millennium!

Pyrotechnics display completes the Millennium celebrations

Appendix 1

DOVER MAYORS AND THEIR TIMES   1945-2000

1945 Arthur Goodfellow. For the first time, Labour controlled Dover Borough Council and Mr Goodfellow, in November, was elected the town's first Labour mayor. He served at a difficult time for four years.

1949 William (Bill) Fish, who died in office, was elected Conservative mayor four times with a change in political control of the borough council and bestowed the Freedom of Dover on wartime prime minister Winston Churchill.

1953 Reginald Snelgrove, farmer and butcher, was mayor during Elizabeth II's Coronation year. He served as mayor for two years.

1955 Sydney F. Kingsland was mayor when a treasure trove of 700 silver coins were discovered in Market Street.

1957 John (Jack) Williams, during his two years in office, welcomed the Hungarian refugees and voted with the Labour opposition to build The Gateway flats on Dover sea front.

1958 Roland Eckhoff, during his two years in office, took part in the sea front celebrations for the 300th anniversary of the Restoration of the Monarchy.

1960 Dorothy Bushell was Dover's first woman mayor and saw the completion of The Gateway flats.

1961 Robert Eade, working for Dover Harbour Board, often walked with the red danger flag in front of the sea front train.

1962 Arthur Husk, owner of a haulage company, saw almshouses under construction off York Street.

1963 Cyril Chilton's term of office saw the demolition of much of the Last Lane area of Dover including Orme's bookshop.

1964 Ada Brazier was mayor during 12 months when there were three mayors. The death in January 1965 of Alderman Edmund Bushell resulted in Mrs Brazier taking over with Alderman John Bushell in post by the end of the 12 months.

1965 John Bushell, a school master, saw the demolition of Snargate Street Methodist Chapel.

1966 Ernest Pittock was mayor during the year that Sir Robert Menzies was installed as Lord Warden of the Cinque Ports.

1967 Harold Carr saw one way traffic introduced in the main street and the devaluation of the pound by the government.

1968 George Aslett, a school master, welcomed Princess Margaret when she named the first car carrying hovercraft at Dover, *The Princess Margaret*.

1969 William (Bill) Muge, a primary school headmaster, welcomed Princess Anne to Dover when she named a hovercraft after herself. It was during his two year mayoralty that the last printing, in Dover, of a newspaper took place (*Dover Express*). Muge House is named after him.

1971 Reginald (George) Lock, an outfitter, witnessed the closure of the Odeon leaving only one cinema in the town and saw the start of the construction of the widened York Street. The last Dover Quarter Sessions were held.

1972 Kathleen Goodfellow, the daughter of a former mayor after whom

Goodfellow Way is named, saw construction begin on the £2 million Burlington House complex in Townwall Street and made the first telephone call from Dover's new automatic telephone exchange.

1973 Peter Bean was the last mayor of Dover before local government re-organisation.

1974 Peter Mee was the first town mayor of Dover, the chairman of the Charter Trustees.

1975 George Ruck, another school master, was mayor when the Prince of Wales Sea Training School closed. He was mayor when the Queen visited Dover to review the troops and saw the postponement of the construction of the Channel Tunnel even though work on it had begun.

1976 Harold Morison, a former Royal Navy Commander, was mayor when the Prince of Wales visited Dover in command of *HMS Bronington*.

1977 Hubert (Bob) Kemp, a Post Office telephone engineer, was mayor during Dover's celebrations for the Queen's Silver Jubilee.

1978 Denis Clayton welcomed the Duke of Kent for the official opening of Dover International Hoverport.

1979 Marie Hart was present when the Queen Mother was installed as Lord Warden of the Cinque Ports.

1980 Joseph Watson had a difficult year when base lending rates soared to 17% and inflation reached 21.8%. The Queen Mother was at St Mary's Church for the dedication of the air sea rescue window.

1981 Edith Hadden saw the painting of the Queen Mother, as Lord Warden, hung in Dover Town Hall.

1982 Royston (Bob) Tant was mayor during the war with Argentina.

1983 Marie Hart, in her second term as mayor, went to Portsmouth for the naming of *HMS Illustrious*, which was adopted by the Cinque Ports.

1984 Michael Farrell was mayor during the pit strike when more than 1,000 police were on duty in East Kent.

1985 James Truelove saw a short list drawn up for who was to build the Channel fixed link.

1986 George (Jimmy) Hood was mayor when the *Herald of Free Enterprise* sank off Zeebrugge with the loss of 193 lives.

1987 Brian Young was mayor when the Royal Victoria Hospital was offered for sale.

1988 Royston (Bob) Tant, in his second term in office, saw the closure of Castlemount secondary school and the opening of Tesco's superstore at Whitfield.

1989 William (Bill) Newman was mayor when the Berlin Wall came down and the IRA blew up barracks at Deal killing 11 Royal Marines.

1990 Lynette (Lyn) Young was mayor when tunnellers from France and England met under the Channel and when the White Cliffs Experience opened.

1991 Jacqueline (Jackie) Hood, wife of Jim, saw the Channel Tunnel under construction and the new A20 being built through Aycliffe.

1992 William (Bill) Newman was mayor when Dover's Bronze Age Boat was discovered. It was his second term in office.

1993 Kevin Mills, a customs officer, was mayor for two years. He established

Dover's real ale festival in his first year and in the second welcomed ex-servicemen to Dover for the World War II 'Frontline Britain' celebrations.

1995 George (Jim) Hood. Dover was granted parish council status during his second term of office.

1996 Lynette (Lyn) Young, during her second term of office, was mayor for the formation of Dover Town Council, regaining rights withdrawn 22 years earlier under local government reorganisation.

1997 Paul Sheldrake resigned for personal reasons during his two year span as mayor during which Dover, with the rest of the country, mourned the death of Princess Diana.

1998 Margaret Sansum, a former Dover nurse, took over and served as mayor for two years. She took part in the successful Millennium celebrations, applied for city status in 1999, met the Home Secretary over asylum seekers and welcomed the Prince of Wales when he visited Dover Museum.

2000 Gordon Cowan, a Royal Mail employee, was also chairman of Town Centre Management Company during his term of office and welcomed the Duke of Edinburgh when he unveiled the Admiral Ramsay statue at Dover Castle.

NB The dates given are the years the mayors were elected. The mayoral year normally spans 12 months beginning in May and therefore continues into the following year.

Appendix 2

SOME OTHER NOTEWORTHY EVENTS

1947 Relic-portion of HMS Codrington towed off Dover beach
1947 32,712 ration books issued to Dover's population
1951 Six Dover men prisoners of war of the Chinese in the Korean War
1952 Royal Naval Minewatching Service formed in Dover
1953 Cinque Ports adopt aircraft carrier HMS Albion
1953 Korean War truce-Dover prisoners of war released
1954 HMS Albion lies off the port on official visit
1954 Dover census of 1951 gives the population as 35,215
1956 Part of Old Folkestone Road was lost in cliff fall near Capel
1957 Dover's population 35,370, is the highest since the war
1958 Queen and Duke of Edinburgh visit Dover
1958 Princess Royal inspects Yorkshire regiment at Dover
1967 Garden in Dover dedicated to Lidice, town razed by Nazis
1971 Pelican crossings in use in Dover
1975 Hurricane force winds hit Dover
1980 Minimum lending rate reached 17 per cent
1983 Temperature in July, "hottest ever," at 32.3 Centigrade
1986 Temperature in February fell to minus 15.4 degrees
1987 Hurricane (105mph) hit Dover – much damage
1992 Anger over £65 community charge (poll tax) increases in Dover
1992 PM John Major rejected George Cross campaign for Dover
1992 Dover Rotary Club took ambulance to Split, Yugoslavia
1993 Grave robbers attacked tombs in Cowgate cemetery.
1994 Controversial bail hostel in Park Avenue closed.
1994 White bellied black dipper bird sighted at Kearsney Abbey
1994 East Kent Fairs' boss David Meyer moved to North Africa
1994 Countess Mountbatten unveiled sea front memorial to war victims
1995 Plans for Dover independent community radio station
1995 Works arm of Dover District Council switched to SITA(GB).
1997 Widow Sally Martin, 70, and sons won £4.7 million in the lottery
1997 Dover memorial services for Diana, Princess of Wales
1998 French market held in Market Square and Cannon Street
2000 Row over Terry Lee's plan to bury wife in his back garden
2000 Prince Charles visited Bronze Age Boat museum
2000 Lorry drivers blockaded petrol depots – car queues at garages
2000 Duke of Edinburgh visited Dunkirk "little ships"

ACKNOWLEDGEMENTS

We wish to thank the following for their help in researching this book

Lionel Bish
Steve Carswell
Chris Collings
Reg Colman
Sylvia Corrall
Dover Express
Dover Library
Dover Mercury
Dover Museum
Allan Edgington
Michael Foad
Jim Francis
Trish Godfrey
Ivan Green

Dennis Hammond
Joe Harman
Ken Horne
Lillian Kay
Christopher Leach
Mike McFarnell
Ken Nye
Keith Parfitt
Peter Pascall
Brian Philp
George Ruck
Michael Sharp
Graham Tutthill
Alan Walker
Francis Watts

and especially May Jones for her proof reading and 'polishing' and
Bob Hollingsbee for researching and providing many of the photographs

BIBLIOGRAPHY

Perambulation of Dover by Bavington-Jones 1907

The Story of the Dover Lifeboats by Jeff Morris

The Book of the Cinque Ports by Ivan Green (Barracuda Books 1984)

The Constitutional History of the Cinque Ports by K M E Murray (Manchester University Press 1935)

Dover's Hidden Fortress by John Peverley (Barracuda Books 1996)

Various Dover Society Newsletters

The Roman Painted House at Dover by Brian Philp (KARU 1985)

Romans in East Kent by Stephen Scoffham (North Kent Books)

Excavation of the Roman Forts of the Classis Britannica at Dover by Brian Philp (KARU 1981)

Roman House with Bacchic Murals at Dover by Brian Philp (KARU 1989)

Archaeology in the Front Line by Brian Philp (KARU 2002)

Play Up Dukies (Old Boys Association of Duke of York's RMS 1986)

The Life and Times of a Dovorian by Lillian Kay (Riverdale Publications 1999)

Dover – Collected Memories of a Century by A F Adams and Merril Lilley (Triangle Publications).

Kent Archaeological Review number 116.

A brief history of Maison Dieu House and Dover's libraries by Keith Howell (KCC 2002)

Historic Dover; Archaeological Implications Survey by David Wilkinson Oxford Archaeological Unit (Dover District Council 1990).

Dover Town Centre Investment Zone Archaeological Appraisal by Keith Parfitt (CAT 1998).

The Industrial Eden by Richard Tilden Sherren. (Channel Publications 1990).

LIST OF ILLUSTRATIONS

Illustrations should not be reproduced without the permission of those shown in italics - the source of the photograph and/or the copyright owner.

Characters

CHAPTER 5 Shops, Offices and Hotels

CHAPTER 6 Industry

Characters

CHAPTER 7 Kent Coal

CHAPTER 8 Education

Characters

CHAPTER 9 Health and Welfare

CHAPTER 10 Law and Order

Characters

CHAPTER 12 Heritage

Characters

CHAPTER 13 Digging Up Dover's Past

CHAPTER 14 Lord Wardens

Characters

CHAPTER 15 Garrison

CHAPTER 16 Churches

CHAPTER 20 Sport

Characters

CHAPTER 21 Channel Swimming

CHAPTER 22 General Elections

Characters

CHAPTER 23 Millennium

INDEX

Please note that organisations named Dover may be found under Dover or without Dover in title.

Bentley, Alf - 162
Berryman, Montague - 85
Betteshanger Colliery - 61,63,64
Biggin Hall - 10
Biggin Street - 10,18,19,39,41,42,43,45,46,48,
    52,102,107,123,149,153
Bish, Lionel - 138
Bishop, Len - 175
Blackman, George - 12
Blashford-Snell, Lt. Col. John - 118
Blenheim Square - 51
BMW - 55
Boldware Gate - 108
Bond, Mr - 66
Booth, J. - 68
Boots the Chemist - 10,39,42,43,123
Bowling League - 162
Boy Scouts - 59,131
Boynton, Adrian - 71,72,137,
Brambley Hedge - 79
Bridge Street - 50,77,153
Britannia PH - 40,154
British Queen PH - 153
British Rail - 23, 25,26,36,40,51
British Rail ferries - 35
British Restaurant - 1
British Sailors' Society - 70
Bronze Age Boat - 14,109,110,186,188
Brook House - 69,77,79,98
Brooks, Peter - 163
Brown House - 39
Brown, Tony - 162
Buckland - 17,50,51,125
Buckland Bridge - 17,18,20,152
Buckland Community Centre - 82
Buckland Estate - 4,5,7,65,67,82,122,148
Buckland Hospital - 18,77,78,79,81,163
    (see also Workhouse)
Buckland Mill Bowling Club - 159
Buckland Paper Mill - 49,57,58
    (see also Wiggins Teape)
Buckland Picture House - 150
Buckland School - 68,69
Buckland Terrace - 124
Budd, Bernard - 175
Burgoyne Heights - 118
Burlington Hotel - 7
Burlington House - 14,42,187
Burr, Arthur - 61
Burton, Carly - 166

Burton's - 40
Bushell, Dorothy - 10,11,176,185
Bushido Society - 162
Bushy Ruff - 82,149
Butchery Gate - 108
Buzzard, John - 85
B-Wise - 46
Byer, Darren - 164

Cafe de Paris - 42
Cage Bird Society - 180
Cairn, Ryan - 79
Camber - 23,30,84
Camden Crescent - 40,45
Campaign for Nuclear Disarmament - 132
Cannon Street - 1,19,45,48,102,149,153,154,188
Canterbury Archaeological Trust (CAT) - 108,110
Canterbury Orchestra - 138
Carlton Club - 40,131
Carnival Committee - 151
Carnival of Planets - 183
Carnival Week - 143,150
Castle Avenue - 68,99
Castle Hill House - 131
Castle Street - 10,45,50,53-55,59,101,149,150
Castlemount School - 65,67,68,70,72,73,161,186
Cause is Altered PH - 153
Caves Cafe - 40
Cedars Hotel - 131
Chamber of Commerce - 40,46
Chandos PH - 154
Channel Swimming & Piloting Association - 174
Channel Swimming Association - 169,171,
    173,180
Channel Theatre - 144
Channel Tunnel - 12,17,20,21,23,26,31,34,55,
    61,82,119,126,156,179,186
Channel Tunnel Company - 32,61
    (see also Eurotunnel)
Channel Tunnel Group - 32
Channel Tunnel Treaty - 32
Chapman, Jane - 176
Charity Darts League - 163
Charlton Centre - 45,46
Charlton Church - 5,87,122,133
Charlton Green - 6,7,39,45,46,49,50,54,56,
    131,153,179
Charlton School - 66
Cheeseman's Head - 29
Cherry Tree Avenue - 17,18,48